The
First-Time
Gardener

The
First-Time
Gardener

Pattie Barron

Crown Trade Paperbacks
New York

Published by Crown Trade Paperbacks, 201 East 50th
Street, New York, New York 10022. Member of the
Crown Publishing Group.

Random House, Inc., New York, Toronto, London,
Sydney, Auckland

CROWN TRADE PAPERBACKS and colophon are trademarks of
Crown Publishers, Inc.

Manufactured in Belgium

Library of Congress Cataloging-in-Publication data is
available upon request

ISBN 0-517-88619-7

10 9 8 7 6 5 4 3 2 1

First American Edition

Project Editor   Anne de Verteuil
Art Editor   Tony Seddon
Picture Research   Claire Taylor
Production   Jill Macey
Visualizer   Lesley Craig
Illustrators   Rachel Ross, Liz Pepperell
Consultant   Cassandra Danz

CONTENTS

INTRODUCTION

Whoever said true gardeners were born with green thumbs? I maintain they're something that you acquire as you practice, in your own way, the supremely satisfying act of gardening. Tools are important. Techniques are too, and I hope you'll find all you need in this starter book to take you through the basics. A decent-sized plot to work on and a few terrific near-by plant nurseries wouldn't harm either. But the first-time gardener's most important quality is enthusiasm, because this leads you to discover new ways to propagate plants, to visit other gardens country-wide – or world-wide – for inspiration, perhaps even (it happens) to the flathills of the Andes as you find that the garden center can no longer satisfy your curiosity about new plants. You will find that with this enthusiasm – which creeps up on you as inevitably as aphids creep up on roses – you never stop learning, discovering, absorbing. And one thing is assured: this garden enthusiasm, which frequently becomes an absorbing passion, will see you right through your life.

STARTING FROM SCRATCH

As well as creators of dreams, good
gardeners are realists, first and foremost.
They know precisely what they've got
to work with: the best of it, and the
worst of it. If a garden is heavily shaded
by trees, there is no point hoping for a
great crop of sunflowers; in fact, there is
no point sowing the seeds in the first
place. Gardeners also know how far to
push nature, and when to back off and
leave things be. In other words, blue
Himalayan poppies may be your idea of
heaven but if you don't have the right
acidic soil – or the dedication, for that
matter – cross them off your list. Don't
mourn them, but concentrate on what
you *can* grow. That probably leaves
only about 60,000 varieties of plants to
choose from, so don't feel too sorry for
yourself. Everyone can have a glorious
plant-packed garden, whatever their
limitations. Poor soil can be vastly
improved; a windy, exposed site can be
made more hospitable; a plant that
needs special soil can be cosseted in a
container with the appropriate compost.
You might even be able to grow that
Himalayan poppy after all. Miracles can
happen, but it's mostly up to you.

GET TO KNOW YOUR GARDEN

The most successful gardens are those which are in sympathy with their surroundings, and have plants which suit the garden's specific conditions. Your garden's location, exposure to the elements, and soil type should all heavily influence your choice of plants.

Before you get to know plants, get to know your garden. Ask yourself the following (and jot down your responses in a wipe-cover notebook because nobody has that good a memory):

HOW EXPOSED IS YOUR GARDEN?

Only the hardiest of plants can stand constant assault from the elements in the form of harsh, drying winds or prolonged and severe bouts of frost in spring and fall. The first-time gardener suddenly finds his ear is cocked for tomorrow's weather report, but you won't need an expert to tell you if your plot suffers batterings from strong winds, which frequently wreak more damage in the garden than frost. At London's famous botanical garden, the Chelsea Physic Garden, pomegranate trees and myrtle bushes positively flourish, but although London's microclimate helps, those high brick walls which surround the garden provide further warmth and shelter.

If your garden is very exposed, consider wind filters such as wattle fencing, pickets, or a shelter belt of tough trees or shrubs. Even a trellis fence planted with climbers can offer considerable wind protection in the small garden, and increase the number of plants you can effectively grow.

It is alternate bouts of frost and thaw, rather than prolonged frost, that do the most harm to plants. They might seem fine, then, during a milder spell, suddenly collapse. Even if you are in a mild part of the country, your garden could still have or be in a frost pocket – a plant-vulnerable dip or hollow where very cold air gathers and lingers, because it is blocked by a barrier and has no escape route. If your garden is on a slope, for instance, and there is a wall at the base of that slope, the resultant

FROST POCKETS

1

2

1 When planting, note that frost rolls down a slope and gathers in the depression.

2 In the same way, frost settles in a hollow when a barrier blocks its route.

dip provides the perfect potential for a frost pocket. Removing a few bricks here and there in the wall for the frost to filter through will help somewhat, but more valuable yet is the knowledge that, despite the soil and sunny aspect in that hollow, those doubtfully hardy plants you're longing to grow are best reserved for the higher slopes. By warm, sunny walls, in sheltered, still corners, or beneath trees are the places for your least frost-tolerant plants. *Know which areas of your garden are susceptible to early and late frost, so that you know where best to site frost-vulnerable or frost-hardy plants.*

WHAT DIRECTION DOES YOUR GARDEN FACE?

The words that make most music to a house-hunting gardener's ears aren't 'rolling acres' or even 'magnificent view' but these: 'garden with a sunny aspect'. (Add the word 'sheltered', and the plantsman is truly in paradise). If your garden faces the direction of the sun you may have little shade, but it means you can grow the widest range of plants, especially as you can create artificial shade with garden structures such as arbors and pergolas for plants that relish a shady situation. A garden with few hours of sunlight provides less warmth and light, but then most gardens have a little of everything, irrespective of the direction they face: full sun at intervals; dappled shade from overhanging trees; deep shade for at least part of the day in one or more areas. Coupled with these diverse factors are areas of the garden which are dust-dry, those which are damp and even boggy because of poor drainage or because they are near an

A windbreak of Rosa rugosa

area of natural water, and gloomy corners which seem unable to accommodate any plants at all (they will, they will). Familiarizing yourself with every part of your plot is vital before you begin planting.

Note, too, which corners of the garden receive low light, and which direct, warming sunlight. This is vital knowledge if certain plants are to flourish. Even in the South, camellias, for instance, won't tolerate the speedy thawing from frost that early morning sun brings if they are sited in a cold, cheerless location, but against a warm wall or fence they won't have to face that stress. Frost-tender climbers best suited to growing under glass can succeed against a sunny wall in the South, but on a less hospitable location, frankly, they won't have a hope. You can grow sweet cherries successfully on a warm wall, but they'll sulk against a wall that doesn't bask in sunshine. However, in cold climates you can grow north star cherries and blueberries (proving my point that there is a corker of a plant for all places).

IN WHAT SORT OF REGION DO YOU LIVE?

Living halfway up a mountain, or on the coast lashed by salty sea breezes, obviously dictates, to an extent, the kind of plants you can expect to grow. Maritime plants and leathery-leaved shrubs, for instance, have foliage and roots that are especially adapted to tolerate those salty onslaughts and tough conditions by the sea; others will simply wither and die. The horticultural advantage of living in an urban, built-up area instead of among rolling rural acres is that all those towering office complexes provide another kind of build-up: warmth and physical protection. City dwellers in their notable microclimates tell proud tales of growing tender pelargoniums (windowbox geraniums) all through the winter, while in the less hospitable reaches of rural areas, bedding plants may survive for the shortest of seasons. However, gardening magazines carry stories of readers in comparatively cold regions, who manage to grow such tropical delights as melons and passionfruit outdoors, which shows that nature is surprisingly accommodating, especially when encouraged by a never-say-die gardener.

11

BASICS: THE TOOLS, THE MATERIALS

THE MUST-HAVES

If you've got a spade, you can dig. Welcome to gardening. (And if you've got muscle, you can double dig, which we'll come to, no point putting you off when you've just begun.) A garden **SPADE** for digging and shifting soil, planting shrubs, and a four-tined garden **FORK** for preparing the soil, aerating the lawn, preparing the planting hole, shifting compost and so on, are the first-time gardener's, and everybody else's, basics. Buy the best you can afford; the clothesaholic's cost-per-wear theory (wearing an expensive, well-made suit 100 times equals ten wearings of a cheap, shoddily made one) holds true in the toolshed too. Stainless steel provides the most effective cutting edge, gleams invitingly and lasts a lifetime. And if you do commit the mortal sin of leaving it out, it will survive to shine again. Try spade or fork before you buy (ignore the strange looks), making length of shaft, and weight, your main considerations. Get what feels most comfortable. No earthly point purchasing a heavy digging spade if it's too heavy for you to lift easily, let alone use; a so-called border spade should fit the bill to start with.

A **TROWEL** for small-scale planting and digging out of obstinate weeds is next on the priority list. Stainless steel versions are affordable and are a better bet than cheap models that tend to bend at the neck. Choose one that doesn't feel too heavy in your hand, and that has a comfortable handle. Partner to the trowel is a **HAND FORK** for weeding.

HAND CLIPPERS for pruning, clipping and deadheading should be stuck in their own holster around your hips as you swagger around your land,

ready for action. Choose between more common bypass clippers, which have a scissor action, and anvil clippers, which have one curved blade that cuts onto a flat edge; I prefer bypass, but the choice is yours. You might need one lightweight pair and one heavier duty, but don't use either to attempt to cut branches or stems larger than they can handle. Even the finest clippers will only make that essential clean stem break when they're sharp, so have them regularly serviced.

Also useful is a **RAKE** with a rigid head for working the soil to the right texture before sowing seeds. (A **SPRING-TINED RAKE**, which has long, angled

TRIED BUT TESTING

Like many gardeners, I've worked my way through gimmicks. Wonder weeders that twist your wrist and leave the weed intact; 'snail motels' that slugs and snails lounge in front of, never inside; springy lawn aerators that have you bounding about like a bunny rabbit when a garden fork will do just as well. I've tried them all. Face the hard fact that there are few short cuts to good gardening techniques, and you will save yourself a lot of money in years to come.

prongs, is useful for gathering leaves and debris from the lawn, if you have one.)

A **DUTCH HOE** is invaluable. It has a front cutting edge so that when you slide it up and down a small patch of earth it will break down the soil surface and cut annual weeds. However, it will also cut the heads off other more interesting seedlings, too. If you fall in love with hoeing – it happens, especially to vegetable growers – consider hoes that cut from two, or three, sides.

A 2 gal (9 litre) capacity **WATERING CAN** is the garden size to go for. The pros use metal, but a water-filled plastic can is lighter. That superlong spout is necessary so that water flow reaches as far as possible. Aside from a hose (unless your plot is hanky-sized), you'll need a small plastic watering can with rose and fine nozzle attachments for container plants and seedlings. Also a spray bottle or two for misting, not just water, but foliar feed and pest spray too.

THE OPTIONALS

The following are all highly useful additions to the basic kit. Aside from these, you'll find you develop your own favorite garden tools. I wouldn't be without an old kitchen knife for scraping up grass blades from paving cracks.

HALF-MOON EDGER This nifty turf chopper, will become indispensable as you make the lawn ever smaller to accommodate wider beds for housing more plants.

LONG-HANDLED PRUNERS OR LOPPERS Long handles provide extra leverage so you can cut thicker stems and branches than you can using clippers. Also very handy, of course, for out-of-reach stems. (Chunky branches need pruning saws).

MAINTENANCE

Leave a metal tool or gardening machinery out in the rain and you'll soon find out what it means to throw money away. Even if there's a thunderstorm threatening and it's started to hail, even if, heaven forbid, you'll miss the beginning of your favorite gardening program on TV, always wipe your tools clean with a damp cloth, dry them thoroughly and then put them away in a dry place. If possible, keep them off the floor, hung up on the wall for choice. You'll thank me in time for this advice.

Another tip: don't be tempted to rinse mud off under the kitchen tap unless you're a accomplished at freeing the U-bend of half a ton of silt. (I know all about this.) Wipe oil frequently over the joins of clippers and shears, as well as the blades. Sharpen blades and cutting edges regularly. Always clean the lawnmower of clippings as much as you can before putting it away, unless you want to spend the rest of your life picking off pieces of dried grass. All types of mower, yours included, need an annual service.

GARDEN SHEARS For cutting hedges and trimming lawn edges. My lawn is so small I use razor-sharp paper scissors! Kinder on the back are long-handled **SCYTHES**; you can buy them with right-angled blades to make the task easier yet.

WHEELBARROW Handy for larger gardens. Worth considering is the space-saving wheelbarrow with collapsible treated fabric carry-all. Small plots can do fine with plastic buckets. When they're not holding grit, garden tools, compost, you name it, they can be stacked like flowerpots.

GARDENING GLOVES I only use fabric gloves when pruning roses. Give me heavy duty rubber gloves any day, though there are jobs for which only bare hands will do. *Note:* even weekend gardeners should have a tetanus shot.

MAJOR MACHINERY

For owners of even a small grassy patch, a **LAWNMOWER** is compulsory. Make your choice from rotary or cylinder mowers, and those that run on

electricity, gasoline (an advantage in that you don't need a cord), or good old-fashioned push-power. New on the market are nifty rechargeable, cord-free mowers. For perfect turfs, cylinder mowers – blades in the cylinder scissor-cut the grass – are the best choice. Bear in mind that baseball field stripes only work on a completely flat, even surface that is completely free of weeds. Rotary mowers have horizontal blades on a whizzing wheel that literally scythe the grass, and are fine for the average lawn, complete with all its lumps and bumps. A hover rotary is perfect for working its way over bigger bumps and banks. Compulsory too is a powerbreaker in case of accidents.

WEED WACKER If you don't mind wearing goggles and protective footwear, you might want one. I don't, but I hate the idea of a cord whistling around my ankles at a twillion twirls a second, and I'm not obessive about neat edges. But the weed wacker has its uses, it can navigate corners and the base of trees, and get into those awkward corners that a lawnmower can't reach.

13

DOING THE GROUNDWORK

Good garden soil is the most important factor of all in successful plant growing. The ideal garden soil is nutrient-rich (finding lots of earthworms – live ones, that is – when you dig is a good sign), has the texture of Dutch apple pie topping, the color of a chocolate brownie, allows water to drain through easily, while retaining enough moisture to provide adequate nutrition for plants.

Listen, I did say the ideal soil, known as loam in proper garden circles. If you're looking despairingly out onto a sea of swamp mud in spring, or worse yet, in summer, take heart. Miracles can be wrought, and as consolation, note that some plants will come through under the most stressful conditions. But as I'm assuming you wish to grow the widest possible range of plants – and have them thrive, not merely survive – you must get your soil into the covetable condition known as being 'in good heart'. This health-giving operation is a lifelong (yours) commitment. Gardeners continue year

Getting to know your soil is the first step to making it work for you. Once you discover whether you're dealing with a fertile but heavy clay, or a light, stony soil that needs feeding, you can start taking action to get it in good heart.

after year to put the goodness back into the soil, which plants take out, adding well-rotted manure, compost and all manner of good things to make their earth nutrient-rich and as hospitable as possible for plants. Great soil is glorious stuff and even smells good.

First step, though, before you get to work, is to know exactly what kind of soil you're dealing with. How to tell? Grab a handful (be brave – take those gloves off). *Now squeeze.* Your soil will conveniently fit into one of the categories below, or more likely be a combination of both, to a lesser or greater degree.

CLAY SOIL

If the squelchy, sticky stuff you're seeing – and feeling – could probably make a set of pottery mugs, you've got heavy clay soil. Before you put your head – or your clay – in an oven, the news is not all bad. Clay soil contains masses of nutrients esssential for healthy plant growth. Roses just adore clay soil, and will give their very best. The less great news: clay soil is difficult (understatement) to dig. Those big clods are near impossible to break down into fine seed-sowing tilth; there just aren't enough air spaces between each tiny particle of earth, and plant roots understandably find it difficult to

SOIL TYPES

1 Squeeze a handful of loam and it will tend to stick together, but still remain crumbly in texture.

2 Clay soil is sticky and the particles cling together, making it easy to mold when squeezed.

3 Sandy soil doesn't hold together, slips through the fingers and may feel gritty.

1

2

3

Certain shrubs like this *Pieris* need an acid soil in order to flourish. If you live in the West and your soil is alkaline, grow lime-haters, in large tubs or containers of special lime-free compost.

pH TESTING KIT

If you want to find out whether your soil is acid or alkaline, you can test its pH quite simply with the aid of an inexpensive kit from the garden center that gauges the acid/alkaline levels.

penetrate. In a hot summer, clay soil bakes so dry that cracks sometimes appear across lawns as well as flowerbeds. In cold wet weather, compacted clay soil produces pools and puddles, and plants – many – that can't tolerate having their roots waterlogged simply don't survive. Walk on clay soil when it's wet, and you compact it even more. Bulbs are just as intolerant of sitting in water the whole winter, and are inclined to rot. (The truly optimistic, of course, would maintain that clay soil retains water superbly.) However, I'm saving the very good news till last: you can dramatically improve this soil. The basic fertility is there, you just need to work on improving the texture.

SANDY SOIL

If the soil simply slides through your fingers, say hello to light, sandy soil (or chalky, for that matter). It is pretty spineless, insubstantial stuff, and in literally sharp contrast to clay, has too many air pockets and too few nutrients. Water goes right through it without lingering, providing little nourishment for plants. Their roots endeavor to grab what nutrients are lurking around, but there's just too little to hang on to. This, too, will pass, provided you put in some serious spadework, incorporating lots of bulky organic matter which will give the soil substance, improve water and nutrient retention, as well as promoting soil fertility.

ACID OR ALKALINE?

You can successfully grow an enormous number of plants without concerning yourself whether your soil is acid or alkaline, but some key plants – notably rhododendrons, azaleas, camellias, pieris, most heathers – will only flourish if they are planted in acid soil. They simply *will not grow* in very

alkaline soil. This is because alkaline and chalky soils have a high lime content which these plants cannot abide. Peaty woodland floors have an acid pH, so woodland plants will be right at home if your soil is on the acidic side. On acid soil, blue hydrangeas are a wonderful rich azure shade, but turn a less desirable pink in alkaline soil; you might as well be aware of it.

Peeking at the plants growing in neighboring gardens will give you an idea of the local soil's pH, but a more accurate method of gauging your own garden soil's acid/alkaline level is to buy a simple soil testing kit from the garden center. The best pH if you want to grow a wide range of plants is between 6 and 6.5, which is slightly acidic; the lower the figure, the more acid the soil.

If your soil is very acidic, and you want to grow vegetables, which can't take up nutrients in such soil, you can up the alkaline level by adding lime, a task you'll probably have to repeat every year. Most soil testing kits indicate the amount necessary for your soil's particular pH level. If you can afford it, use calcified seaweed, which lasts longest in the soil and has trace elements; otherwise ask at the garden center for magnesian or Dolomite lime. Wear protective clothes, including a face mask, and don't lime at the same time as applying manure or garden compost; best lime time is late winter or spring.

If you are set on growing acid-loving plants and your soil tests alkaline, instead of trying to change the soil's pH artificially (which never works in the long-term), grow these plants in containers with special ericaceous (lime-free) compost, and water them with distilled, not tap water.

15

GETTING THE SOIL IN GOOD SHAPE

An annual spring dressing of well-rotted manure or garden compost makes a good conditioner, helping to open up and lighten heavy clay soils, as well as adding vital moisture-retaining bulk to thin, stony and sandy soils.

HOME-MADE COMPOST Without any doubt, the most satisfying way of adding goodness to the soil, household waste is recycled back into the earth as rich, crumbly, beneficial compost. Good reason enough surely for the smallest plot to find room for a compost bin (*for more details see p. 20*).

LEAFMOLD If your garden is within direct firing line of overhanging trees, rejoice. In autumn, gather up the fallen leaves (they must be moist), shove them in big bin bags, push down firmly and seal the bags, making a few perforations in each. If you've got the space for a more permanent leafmold composter, bang four posts into the ground and wrap wire netting around them. After one year, preferably two, you'll have brown, crumbly leafmold, an excellent soil conditioner.

MAKING LEAFMOLD

Turn fallen leaves into a rich soil conditioner by stacking them in a leafmold composter. Simply bang four posts into the ground, wrap wire netting around them, tip in your autumn leaves, and wait a year or two.

Good, workable soil is a well-aerated mixture of clay, sand or grit and humus, which is not a Greek appetizer but decomposed organic matter that greatly increases the fertility of the soil. Humus is far more beneficial to your earth – and to plants – than scattering fertilizer all over the place. Humus feeds all life forms that exist in the soil and these in their turn work on improving soil structure; humus activates sluggish earth and brings it to life.

All soil types benefit from the addition of humus. To light soil it adds much-needed bulk, improves texture, and helps to retain moisture; incorporated into heavy soil it improves drainage and makes it less compacted.

SOIL IMPROVERS

Incorporate humus into the soil with at least one of the following. Well-rotted manure and home-made compost are the top organic soil improvers.

WELL-ROTTED HORSE OR COW MANURE This adds most fertility to the soil, as well as bulk. Find a local source of the genuine stuff, fork it up yourself, and look on this operation as your baptism as a gardener!

Scan local newspapers for ads, ask nearby farms, ask other gardeners, ask at riding stables and race tracks where horses are stabled. Make sure it is well-rotted, i.e. has been lying for at least a year, as fresh manure is too strong for direct use and may also be contaminated.

MULCHES

A black plastic mulch laid on a bare plot will suppress emerging weeds. To plant through the plastic, slash a cross shape and turn in the four points to form a square.

Keep ground around shrubs clear of weeds by applying an ornamental mulch of coarse bark chippings 2in (5cm) thick. Leave a gap between mulch and the plant's stems.

SPENT MUSHROOM COMPOST Buy bags at the garden center. Don't use if your soil is alkaline, as the lime content will tip the balance further, or with acid-loving plants. However, some companies have started to measure the lime content before selling, so check first before you decide.

SPECIALS FOR CLAY Washed grit bought in bulk from builders' suppliers, and forked into clay soil, is invaluable in opening up the compacted texture. Limestone chippings will make the soil more alkaline. Plants such as lavenders, pinks and rosemary, which thrive on well-drained, stony soil, will benefit greatly from extra grit forked into clay soil before planting.

PEAT OR PEAT-SUBSTITUTES Peat as a soil improver is ineffectual, and as its sources are becoming limited, suitable alternatives should be sought whenever possible. Manufacturers of garden products are wising up to the growing concern about using peat and are focusing on industry by-products instead. Keep a look out for enterprising and effective soil improvers that are composted blends of one or more of the following: sawdust, coconut fiber, bark, paper, shells, sunflower husks, fruit fiber.

HOW TO APPLY SOIL IMPROVERS

Dig or fork over the soil – autumn and winter are the best months. About a bucketful for every yard (meter) is enough. There is no need to break your back deep-digging: just work it into the top layer of soil, where it is most needed. Leafmold is best forked onto the surface, as a mulch.

THE MARVEL OF MULCH

Good gardeners cover their soil with a thick coverlet of organic matter, at least 2in (5cm) deep, for all manner of reasons, outlined below. All soil improvers can be applied as a mulch. Watchpoint: keep bases of shrubs and trees clear of mulch to avoid rot, and whatever type you choose, make sure it is composted first, or it will rob the soil of valuable nitrogen as it breaks down to humus.

MULCH AS WATER RETAINER
Mulches applied when the earth is moist will help keep that moisture in the soil, and in summer will minimize water evaporation from soil. Result: plants establish faster, grow more healthily, and are less likely to die in a drought.

MULCH AS WEED SUPPRESSANT A thick layer of mulch will shut light out and therefore help to suppress the growth of weeds, which like all plants need light to survive. To clear a bare plot of weeds a season before planting, lay thick black perforated plastic sheeting or old carpet over the ground; early spring, when weeds are just starting up, is the best time. Conceal plastic with a layer of bark chippings if the area is on display. Several layers of newspaper covered with soil make another effective weed suppressant, and when the mulch has served its purpose, you can fork it into the soil as an improver.

17

TO DIG, OR NOT TO DIG

Double digging consists of digging to the depth of two spits, which is equal to the length of the spade blade (a spit), times two. Some gardeners feel they haven't done the job properly unless they double dig the ground (which is doubly difficult if the ground is filled with plants already). But the terrific news is that this back-breaking technique is only really necessary if you need to break up the most unyielding of ground for the first time (and trust me, you won't be burning to do it again). You might have to double dig, for instance, if builders have left your brand new garden plot with tightly compacted soil, or if you are preparing a vegetable plot for the first time. In the opposite camp to the double diggers, there are some gardeners who don't dig at all, but regularly mulch the earth with humus and let it sink into the soil to work its goodness, which is good gardening practice, too. However, single digging is a necessary and manageable gardening task which aerates and prepares soil for annual vegetable and flower plots. As you go (slowly, slowly), you can also pull out the nastiest of weeds and dig in organic matter, and possibly fertilizer, too. Forget the sight

SINGLE DIGGING

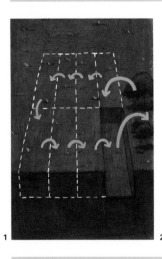

1 Over the plot you want to cultivate, mark out a series of equal sized trenches with your spade.
2 Dig out first trench to the depth of your spade, and about 12in (30cm) wide. Leave soil lying alongside.
3 Dig second trench as first, but turn the soil into the trench in front. Continue as marked in Fig 1, until the first trench is filled with soil from the last.

DOUBLE DIGGING

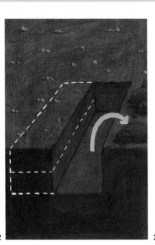

1 and **2** As for single digging, but dig out trench to a width of 24in (60cm) and 2 spades' depth, keeping soil from each spit separate. Fork over base of trench and work in well-rotted manure or compost.
3 Dig second trench, turning soil from upper spit of second trench to base of first, and soil from lower spit of second trench to top of first. If topsoil is less than two spits deep, turn lower spit soil into trench first, and then upper spit soil on top, so that top and subsoil are not mixed.

18

of sumptuous flower beds and rose arbors: there is nothing like seeing a patch of freshly turned, weed-free earth to make a gardener's heart sing with satisfaction and accomplishment. And if you dig your plot in autumn, those rough clods of freshly turned earth will further be broken down by the frosts and thaws of winter.

TOPSOIL: TEEMING WITH LIFE!

The first-time gardener's determination to plumb the depths with his or her shiny new spade, in the belief that he is doing a good thing is worthy but misguided. All the goodness of the earth – the fertility, the fungi, the animal life, you name it – is contained in the topsoil, the uppermost layer. It is this topsoil that nourishes and nurtures plants, and where they put down their young roots; the subsoil beneath is more compacted and far less fertile, so should interest you as little as it interests the majority of your plants. Leave it be, and focus your good intentions on the topsoil. You can easily tell topsoil from subsoil because they are different colors. If you're lucky, your topsoil will be as

SOIL CROSS SECTION

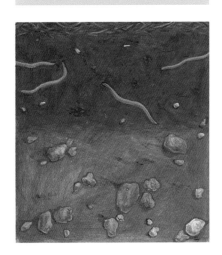

deep as 3ft (1m), but it could be a lot less. Whatever the depth, your topsoil is where the party is happening, and it's up to you to make it a sensation.

ORGANIC GARDENING: THE WAY TO GROW

Only several years ago, organic gardeners were a small minority of the gardening population. The feeling was that they grew mainly fruit and vegetables and weren't too concerned about how plants looked. These alternative practitioners used seemingly cranky methods to keep pests from their crops, and made strange concoctions from weeds and worse, for fertilizers.

Now mainstream gardeners – ornamental, vegetable and otherwise – are adopting organic methods of gardening, basically because they make great sense. Consider these organic basics: encouraging the fertility of soil; choosing disease-resistant roses rather than fighting blackspot and mildew with chemicals; laying physical traps and not laying down pellets that can kill pets as well as pests; keeping down weeds with physical, not chemical barriers. And besides, who wants to eat garden produce that has been sprayed to within an inch of its life?

One of the cornerstones of organic gardening is the adoption of preventive measures instead of rushing in after the damage has been done. Above all, organic gardening is about giving the garden back to nature – under your disciplining hand, of course – so that the natural balance of things (for every pest there is a predator, for every plant a pollinator) is restored as much as possible. This, in turn means, not getting crazed about every passing pest's calling card.

It is because organic gardening is more about good garden practice than

CLIPPINGS
✂ Always wear sturdy boots when digging. The correct way to push a spade into the ground? Use the instep, never the ball of the foot.

any passing trend that it is incorporated into gardening technique throughout this book. Gardening organically takes time *but it works*, and produces healthy, vigorous plants. (Compare it to eating right with snacking on junk food.) Certainly, chemical products should only be reached for as a last resort, and used as little as possible. Ultimately, organic gardening not only benefits the environment – a worthwhile cause in itself – but the vitality of your garden and the life it generates.

YOUR COMPOST CORNER

I'm a compost convert, but then what could be more satisfying than turning waste and scraps into a do-good heap of humus? Plants take goodness from the soil, so putting back goodness into the soil sets up a nifty little ecosystem. There is a knack to making compost, because if you simply load up old waste you'll end with a load of old garbage. Follow a few clear compost-making rules, however, and you'll be recycling kitchen, garden and greengrocer parings into a beneficial afterlife of dark, crumbly compost, reminiscent of sweet-smelling fruit cake, that you can slather on the earth to condition the soil and increase its fertility. You'll also be able to sieve it to use in your own potting compost, use it as a beneficial mulch, and throw neat handfuls into planting holes. Let me tell you, baking bread is one thing, but until you've created compost, and seen how it can perk up your garden, you don't know the *meaning* of smug.

19

LET'S TALK ROT

First, find your container, big as your garden can take. It needs to be at least 3ft 6in (1m) square because a small heap just won't generate enough heat to rot down. It needs a lid to retain heat and keep out rain (you could even use thick carpet topped with plastic), and there should be no holes at the sides. A base isn't necessary because you plonk it straight on the earth, raised with a few bricks or wooden planks so air can circulate underneath. Roomy, slatted wooden boxes are fine, but my choice is a specially constructed bin that has insulated walls, because the hotter the heap, the faster you'll get compost (in a matter of months). When you find your compost container, take two, because when one bin is rotting down, the other is heating up; waste not, want not. If you can't find the space for two, use compost from the bottom of the pile and add fresh material to the top.

Unless you're eager to show the world how green you are, you'll want your compost corner in an unobtrusive pocket of your plot. You might even be able to disguise it with trellis and drape honeysuckle over it. Or how about that drab spot behind the garden shed?

NO WASTE IS WASTED WASTE What goes on the heap? Anything vegetable or mineral that's had a life, or comes under the heading organic, qualifies. Keep a bucket in the kitchen – not very elegant, but real gardening isn't – and get into the compulsive habit of chucking everything from tea bags to eggshells, veggie peelings and coffee grounds into it. Shredded newspaper, if you have the patience, can go in too. You can even cut up old clothes as long as they are made of natural fibers.

Outside, you'll find that even the smallest garden offers rich pickings for the compost heap. All your prunings – you'll have loads of them in spring and autumn, especially – and all the spent flowers of summer will go in, along with end-of-season bedding and, of course, grass clipppings. Grow a buddleia, which is chopped practically to the ground every spring, and even just using the soft green prunings, you've got compost for life.

You'll know you're hooked when you can't wait for the hollyhocks to keel over, and you save a mineral-rich banana skin for ages in your pocket (it'll remind you it's there eventually). From that point, it's but a short step to growing things specifically *for* the compost heap, such as the comfrey plant which is rich in nutrients. Some organic gardeners grow potash-rich sunflowers especially to boost the nutrition count in compost.

WHAT TO LEAVE OUT Cooked foods, meat and fish and bones, because you don't want scavengers like rats, thanks very much. Diseased plants, fruits or anything else. Bacteria prefer alkaline conditions, so acidic apples, lemons, tomatoes and potatoes should be limited, although it's not likely you'll be hurling them on whole. Perennial weeds or those that are about to deposit their seed all over the place (if in doubt, leave them out, burn them or bin them.) Woody prunings that will take forever to rot down.

COMPOST SPECIALS TO ADD You can buy commercial activators and accelerators that contain nitrogen, which speeds up the compost process; better still is an effective organic activator that includes herbs, honey and seaweed. Comfrey, nettles, liquid

COMPOST BIN

It makes sense to have two compost bins working for you at the same time, both with waste at different stages of decomposition. That way, you can keep storing in one, while you're taking from the other.

Compost bins are a valuable, not a visual asset to your garden, so it's best to keep them in an out of the way or unobtrusive corner where they won't distract the eye from the more decorative elements.

seaweed, even human urine, all make effective natural activators, as does a handful of ready-rotted compost from a previous heap. Horse manure adds bulk and nutrients. Throw on a handful of night crawlers, from fishing tackle shops, and leave them to multiply and become permanent welcome residents that work their wiggly way up and down the heap, digesting it and thus helping to break it down.

COMPOSING COMPOST: ASSEMBLY IS ALL! Break up bulky waste before throwing it on the heap, and shred or chop prunings small. In lieu of a shredder, I hover over my heap like a Macbeth witch, chopping up prunings with paper scissors or clippers as they hit the heap. I've even heard of a compost freak chopping up kitchen waste in her blender for super-speedy results!

The secret of success is to alternate material in layers of contrasting textures. Too many grass clippings will produce a slimy mess so keep them to thin layers and balance them with thicker, coarser stuff, or mix with shredded newspaper. Straw, too, moistened first, will add bulk to an excess of fresh green material. Garnish layers every so often with earth, blood, fish and bonemeal, seaweed, manure or activator to encourage bacteria. Keep the heap moist and, if you can, turn it after a couple of months to aerate it and thereby speed things up a little. I find this too tricky to manage, but the heap turns to crumbly, devil's-food-cake compost just the same.

COMFREY AND NETTLE TONICS
Home-made liquid feeds can be messy and smelly, but are potent. Russian comfrey is worth growing – though once established, it's hard to get rid of – because it's rich in the three key plant nutrients, nitrogen, phosphorus and potash. Once you have established a comfrey patch, you will be able to cut the large leaves several times a year. You can use comfrey in layers on the compost heap, dig the leaves into the soil or use them as a surface mulch. To make a rich liquid feed for plants, fruits and vegetables, pack the leaves into a plastic bucket and let them ferment into a black liquid, which takes about three weeks. If you use a water barrel, you can drain off the liquid through the tap at the bottom. Too strong to use undiluted, comfrey liquid must be watered down until it is a more plant-palatable weak tea color. You can follow the same method with Scotch thistles, which are purported to increase disease resistance, and mix the two together for an effective organic cocktail.

GREEN MANURE If you can spare the ground for at least six weeks, try this method of fertilizing soil and improving its structure. It's particularly useful as a preliminary to vegetable growing. Sow a green crop (agricultural lupins, buckwheat, clover, vetches or winter rye grass are all suitable) and dig the plants back into the earth while they're young. A word of advice: don't sow more than you can dig in. If you leave the crops too long, you'll have a nightmare patch of tough invaders to get rid of.

WORM COMPOST

Don't let me put you off if your idea of fun is catering for 3,000 red wigglers that all seem to try and wriggle out of their bin every time you take the lid off to feed the little darlings. I know about this, and I'm still having nightmares. Even if you're not as queasy as me, worm bins (the kit consists of a can of worms plus a lidded garbage bin with a drip tray at the bottom to collect liquid compost) can only take a small amount of material at a time. But persevere, and I am assured that the caviar of liquid composts can be yours, but on a very small scale.

21

THE PLANTS

Selecting plants for your garden involves more than going to the garden center and pointing to ones that take your fancy. Choosing a curry plant because it smells invitingly of Indian take out (truly, it does) and a berry-loaded holly because the label pleads forlornly 'Needs a male' are not the best reasons to buy, and can result in good money thrown on the compost heap (take it from one who knows). Of course you need to like your plants, but just as importantly, they need to suit the site/soil/aspect you have in mind for them. In a large garden you can point out the woodland walk in springtime, then divert visitors to the herbaceous border come summer, while the woodland walk kicks its heels. The small garden has no such luxuries, but must look good all year round, with the show continuing smoothly through the seasons. Therefore every plant must have enough plus points – good foliage, autumn hips, whatever – to earn its keep. The plants on the following pages are some of the best possible choices; get to know them before going on to discover many more.

PLANT TYPES

A well-packed garden will consist of many different plants: evergreen and deciduous shrubs and trees, perennials and annuals, biennials and bulbs, many of which should hit their peak at varying times to provide an effective show all the year round.

BARE FACTS

The first-time gardener looks around his recently planted plot and asks anxiously, 'Why are all the leaves falling off my new plants? Why is everything dying on me?' The answer is, of course, that it is fall. (This might sound like an exaggeration, but at some late-season point you'll find yourself tch-tching about foliage fall on a treasured plant, before the truth dawns.) The fact is if you plant only deciduous trees and shrubs – those that lose their leaves – you're in for a dreary winter display, though the autumn tints might well be sensational. If your garden is on view year-round, you might equally be tempted to choose only evergreens – and evergrays – which, believe me, will give you a boring, never-altering display.

Watching the seasons change in his own patch is one of the gardener's great pleasures and unless it snows on the forever green and gold conifers of the evergreen garden, this particular pleasure will be denied its owner.

Aim then for a balance of evergreen and deciduous trees, shrubs and climbers that will display their best points at different times of the year. Once you've established this framework, infill with the plants that have a briefer season: the hardy perennials, temporary bedders and bulbs.

HOW DOES YOUR GARDEN GROW?

You can, I hope, tell a tree from a bulb, but you may not be familiar with some of the other plant categories. If you know how the plants in your garden behave – which ones die down in winter, which flower in their second year, and so on – you're halfway to knowing how to look after them. These are the chief categories:

SHRUBS grow from several woody stems which produce a framework of branches. Examples of evergreen shrubs are *Mahonia* (Oregon grape holly), lavender and holly; deciduous shrubs include winter-flowering jasmine, fuchsia and forsythia.

TREES grow from only one woody stem, although occasionally they can have more. Size cannot be used to define a tree, as there are shrubs – rhododendrons, for example – that can grow larger than some trees.

PERENNIALS are plants which continue to grow year after year. Some are evergreen, like *Bergenia cordifolia*, but most are herbaceous, which means that they die down completely in winter, and send up new shoots in spring. Examples of herbaceous perennials are delphinium, *Aconitum* (monkshood), Japanese anemone. Most perennials are hardy, but **TENDER PERENNIALS** are planted out as summer bedding and are not frost-tolerant; their future is assured by moving them under glass for the winter, or taking cuttings. Examples are begonia, window box geraniums, osteospermum.

ANNUALS are plants which give their all in one year – germinating, flowering, producing seed – then die, so that you enjoy them for just one season. Hardy annuals (clarkia, sweet pea, candytuft, love-in-a-mist) are frost-tolerant so can be planted out earlier in the year than half-hardy annuals

MAKE MINE MALVA MOSCHATA

All right, I could have said musk mallow, and it would have meant exactly the same (though you might have been less impressed). So why Latin names? Because there are so many similar plant varieties, and the Latin terminology, the botanists' universal lingo, allows us to be 100 per cent precise about which plant we are describing. The many varieties of *Salvia* (sage) for instance, would have you screaming if you tried to describe them in English: 'big blue with long stems'; 'red flower and divided leaves', and so on.

Latin botanical names are used internationally, meaning you can communicate with gardeners all over the world. How does it work? Back to *Malva moschata*. The first name describes the genus, telling us that it's from the mallow clan. (There's another type of mallow called *Lavatera*, so you see the need for Latin!) The second name describes the species: *moschata*, or musk. (And if the two names are joined by an x, that signifies the plant is a hybrid, the result of interbreeding

between two species of the same family.) Sometimes a third name is added, which is not Latin, but denotes the name given by the breeder to the cultivar – the cultivated variety – that he has developed from the species. For an example, take *Acer palmatum* 'Osakazuki'. *Acer* = maple; *palmatum* = the species of maple (i.e. palm-shaped leaves, like a hand); 'Osakazuki' is the catchy name given to this particular cultivar. In the same way, a popular fuchsia cultivar is called less elegantly, 'Mrs Popple'.

I never learned Latin, but even to me some of the plant names are surprisingly user-friendly. You don't need to be a Latin scholar to figure out that *Hydrangea serrata* indicates the hydrangea has serrated leaves, that *Cotoneaster microphyllus* describes a small-leaved cotoneaster, or that *Thymus vulgaris* indicates the common form of thyme. Pretty soon you'll be raving about the blossom on your *Prunus* x *subhirtella* 'Autumnalis Rosea' (winter-flowering cherry) without drawing breath.

average garden – certainly trees, shrubs, roses, and most perennials and bulbs – are hardy, i.e. will withstand temperatures below freezing, and can be left out all winter. If a plant is labelled half-hardy, it will need protection against the coldest weather, and if it is tender, like a greenhouse plant, you had better haul it indoors until warmer spring weather, or you'll be sorry.

SPECIES AND CULTIVARS: WHAT'S THE DIFFERENCE?

Nearly all garden plants are hybrids or cultivars of wild plants called species. They are bred under controlled conditions with the aim of improving on the original. Many species shrubs, trees and roses are far too large or ungainly to be of use in our gardens, whereas the cultivated varieties tend to be more compact in growth, and have larger flowers and improved color; a case in point is *Rosa moyesii*, whose cultivar 'Geranium' is more garden-friendly than the original: smaller, better flowering, a sharper shade of scarlet.

(petunia, gazania), which are raised in a greenhouse and planted out after all danger of frost is passed.

BIENNIAL describes plants that live for two years. They produce foliage in the first season, flower the following year, then die. The seeds of biennials can be sown outdoors in summer. Examples are *Digitalis* (foxglove), *Dianthus barbatus* (sweet william).

A **BEDDING PLANT** describes an annual or biennial that is planted in a group simply to create a one-season show, such as *Erysimum cheiri* (the biennial wallflower).

BULBS are, quite simply, bulbous plants. Each have their own fleshy storehouse that lies dormant underground until its flowering season. Examples are daffodil, tulip, lily. Also belonging to the bulb family are corms (crocus, gladioli), rhizomes (iris, canna) and tubers (begonia, ranunculus).

HOW HARDY IS HALF-HARDY?

All plants fall into one of three broad divisions, enabling you instantly to assess their frost tolerance: hardy, half-hardy and tender. Most plants in the

Bulbs are invaluable in adding secondary color and structure to a planting. Here, emerging hybrid lilies provide exciting contrast to mauve *Campanula persicifolia* and *Anchusa azurea* 'Loddon Royalist'.

MAKING DECISIONS

Backdrops can make or mar your plants, so consider them carefully. Clapboard painted icing pink looks twice as luscious when studded with the blooms of a climbing rose chosen to complement the color.

WORK WITH WHAT YOU HAVE

Few of us start with a completely bare piece of land to be planted up. Ready-present features – restrictions, even – help bring out the creative side of a person, and push a garden to more exciting frontiers. A shade-giving tree could kick off a woodland bed; an unforgiving red brick wall could be painted ice-pink to site a crimson climbing rose, and a knockout crane's bill geranium that's been happily growing in the garden for years, flattering every neighboring plant, should be left exactly where it is. As a first-time gardener I had fixed ideas about what I wanted growing in my personal space. For some reason one of the most gorgeous and floriferous crane's bill geraniums, 'Johnson's Blue', didn't qualify, so I spent much time endeavouring to pull it out completely, a fruitless exercise because it was growing from a crack in between stone steps. Thankfully, another virtue of 'Johnson's Blue' is that it is fairly indestructible, and it remains one of my garden's stalwarts.

Missionary zeal tends to overcome the first-time gardener. He/she must have the best, brightest and biggest plants. When confronted with green or variegated or golden, the latter two win out with the starter gardener, although he finds out in time that the variegated will frequently revert back to plain, or be less hardy than the plain, or else the gold will get scorched by frost and not grow as sturdily as the plain. The same is true of double flowers: double might be twice as nice, but often only flowers half as well. The first-time gardener reasons, why have a blue geranium when you can have a shocking pink one? Rip out the boring blue one!

Why not pull out a tree? I'll tell you why. Because you'll never do it yourself: it's a major job. Besides, trees give a garden character and – more important – a sense of time. I did, however, when I moved to my current garden (enthusiastic gardeners move to new gardens, not new homes), have a sumach tree, *Rhus typhina*, removed, not because I didn't like the rich red foliage, but because I didn't like the sumach suckers that were coming up like daisies all over the lawn; why ask for trouble? Point is, unless it's a really big negative, something that's going to constantly annoy you, it's best to leave it be. Instead, try some creative tricks. For instance, if you don't like the color of that humdrum lemon climbing rose you inherited with the house, zap it up with large blue-flowered clematis 'Côte d'Azur'. By the same token, less than thrilling shrubs can be enlivened with, say, a perennial sweet pea threaded through them, or merely used as green backdrops to livelier, more colorful candidates. And be realistic. A cottage garden will never be a Japanese garden if you've already got a ranch house, six honeysuckles and some roses, but you could always add an acer or an azalea in an oriental glazed pot near the house.

WHAT MAKES A PLANT GARDEN WORTHY?

Plant space is precious, don't waste it. Before buying a plant check out its key features (an advantage of buying pot-grown plants from garden center or nursery is that you can see them in their full flowering glory). Is it evergreen or deciduous? How long is the plant's flowering period – two weeks or two months? Does it look good without its flowers? Is the foliage interesting? Does it have berries/fruit/colored bark? Will it sprawl everywhere or stay compact? Lilacs, for instance, are glorious for a notoriously short spell; go on vacation in late spring, and you miss the whole show. Unless you can't live without them, cross lilacs off the list, or indulge your love of lilacs with a dwarf variety such as *Syringa vulgaris* 'Nadezhda'. By contrast, the medium-sized shrub *Choisya ternata* 'Aztec Pearl' provides striking, finely cut green foliage all year round, is fairly indestructible, forms a shapely bush, and in early summer is covered with masses of sweetly scented white flowers. You really couldn't ask for more.

DON'T BE A PLANT SNOB

It's easy to become a plant snob as you get to know the more unusual specimens, but many plant snobs are mere plant collectors, not makers of gardens, and their plots tend to look like cheerless specimen beds. Truth is, the reason you see many of the same plants again and again at garden centers is because they consistently perform well and have much to offer both weekend gardener and serious plantsperson. After all, it is how you put plants together and where you place them that makes the magic, not just the plants themselves.

Pyracantha (firethorn) is one of the most common wall shrubs, but it is none the less valuable for that. Tough and undemanding, it provides evergreen foliage, small white flowers and best of all, masses of berries to enliven the autumn garden.

WORKHORSE SHRUBS

When you start out, what you don't want is temperament. The following are some shrubs that give a lot, yet expect little in return. They won't necessarily provide you with center-stage dramatics, but all will prove to be, at least, staunch background supporters. All are hardy in reasonable situations.

For pruning methods A, B and C, see Chapter 3, p. 58.

BERBERIS (barberry) Most berberis have thorny stems, so are good planted in places to deter intruders. They have other assets: a tolerance of soil and site, except for deep shade, and value as foliage as well as flowering shrubs. Flower clusters in spring are shades of rich yellow to deep orange. Evergreen varieties have glossy, dark green leaves and are much used for hedging. *Best Bet*, evergreen: *B. darwinii*, 8ft (2.40m) with small holly-like olive green leaves, tangerine-colored flowers, deep blue berries later. *Best Bet*, deciduous: *B. thunbergii* 'Rose Glow', 5ft (1.5 m) with pink marbled burgundy leaves. *Pruning C.*

BUDDLEIA (butterfly bush) See how buddleia thrives in parking lots, embankments, any old place, and you can see its tenacity. Its only demand is sun. Neglect buddleia, and its a third-rate, untidy shrub; prune dead branches back at winter's end, feed in spring and summer, and you have a border star. In high summer, massive flower spikes are honey-scented; bees and butterflies are nuts about the nectar. Buddleia can soon reach 10ft (3m) and beyond, and is perfect if you want a full-grown shrub in one season.

Best Bets: B. davidii varieties such as 'Black Knight', deep claret flowers; 'Pink Pearl', rosy-lilac flowers; compact 'Lochinch', with gray-green leaves and orange-eyed lavender flowers. *Pruning B.*

CAMELLIA Glossy evergreen bushes produce the showiest of pink, white or red blooms from early to late spring in the warm South – even in late winter, in mildest areas. But camellias only thrive on neutral or acid soil. If your soil is alkaline, consider growing them in a raised bed filled with lime-free topsoil, or in tubs of ericaceous compost. Give them shelter in sun or light shade, ideally against a wall where, early sun after a frost will not damage flowers or foliage. Pamper them with rainwater and tea leaves – they're worth it.

Best Bets: varieties of *C. japonica* or *C.* x *williamsii*, with bushy growth of 5-7ft (1.5-2m), such as 'Chang Temple', pink flowers, semi-double; 'Anticipation', red, peony-like flowers; 'Lion Head', pink-and-red striped. *Pruning C.* Cut out weedy branches after flowering.

CEANOTHUS (blue myrtle) Fast-growing evergreen with small, rounded, glossy leaves for areas south of Washington, DC. Must have sun, but otherwise undemanding, with little or no pruning necessary. And now for the big news: in late spring, the bush is one big mass of blue flowers. Ceanothus gives its best when sited against a warm wall, but in steadily warm climates, can be grown as a free-standing bush.

Best Bets, reliably hardy: *C.* 'Puget Blue', 6ft (1.8m), with trusses of soft blue flowers; *C. thyrsiflorus repens*, low-growing horizontal spreader with sky blue flowers, delicious tumbling over wall or bank. *Pruning C.*

CHAENOMELES (Japanese quince) In sun or shade, in any reasonable soil, chaenomeles produces pink, white or red saucer-shaped blooms on bare branches in early spring, then chunky golden fruit in autumn. Who cares if it's less than special in summer? Grow it as

Ceanothus impressus 'Puget Blue'

Choisya ternata 'Aztec Pearl'

Cytisus x *praecox* 'Allgold'

Chaenomeles looks particularly stunning when set against this backdrop of an old stone wall. When the springtime bloom is over, there's another season of interest as the unusual, quince-like golden fruits continue the display.

Then in summer, you can enjoy the chunky yellow flower spikes that smell of pineapple. *Pruning A*.

FORSYTHIA Justly popular deciduous shrub for backs of borders, though not the last word in graceful growth. In early spring, flashy golden yellow flowers deck the leafless stems to add a dollop of much-needed sunshine. Forsythia tolerates part shade, but flowers best in full sun.

Best Bet: *F.* x *intermedia* 'Lynwood', up to 10ft (3m), fat, golden, four-petalled flowers. *Pruning A*.

HIBISCUS SYRIACUS (Rose of Sharon) Despite its exotic appearance, this summer-flowering deciduous shrub is winter hardy and will thrive in either sun or shade, gowing to a height of 12ft (3.6m). It is also very tolerant of city conditions. You may think it has died on you over winter, but be patient, because it leafs out late.

Best Bets: 'Blue Bird' is almost true blue; 'Diana' has pure white six-inch flowers; 'Pink Giant' has soft pink flowers with a red center and yellow stamens. *Pruning C*.

hedging, free-standing in the border, or even against a house wall or fence.

Best Bets for fences: wide spreading *C. speciosa* varieties such as white 'Nivalis', 8ft (2.5m), lower-growing red 'Simonii'; *Best Bet* for borders: rich red *C.* x *superba* 'Crimson and Gold'. *Pruning A*. For wall-trained plants, cut out branches growing towards, and away from, the wall. For shrubs, thin out crowded branches.

CHOISYA TERNATA (Mexican orange blossom) Californian native evergreen with glossy, oval leaves and a profusion of white flowers in spring; performs best in sunny, sheltered spot. Terrific in pots.

Best Bet for borders: aside from *C. ternata*, new variety 'Aztec Pearl' is a foliage asset; rich green leaves are sharply dissected. *Pruning C*.

CYTISUS (broom) In summer, broom is merely a bunch of green whippy stems, but in spring, when covered with masses of pea flowers in soft creams, buttery yellows, and in some hybrids, pinks, rich reds and purples, broom becomes a graceful, thrilling beauty. Flowers like crazy in a sunny site and well-drained, light soil.

Best Bets: creamy *C.* x *praecox* 'Warminster', 5ft (1.5m) and *C.* x *p.* 'Allgold', with rich yellow flowers. Only be tempted by *C. battandieri* (Moroccan broom), which reaches 15ft (4.5m), if you have a sheltered, sunny spot.

Hydrangea macrophylla 'Mme E. Mouillère'

29

CLIPPINGS

HYDRANGEA These much-loved deciduous shrubs flower in late summer, when most shrubs have given their best. They offer good foliage and large blooms which may be massive mopheads or daintier flatter lacecaps. The flowerheads change color as autumn progresses, and dry beautifully on the stem, to add character to the winter garden. To perform at peak, hydrangeas need rich, moisture-retentive soil and semi-shade.

Best Bets, 3 to 8ft (1-2.5m): *H. macrophylla*; *H. m.* 'Nikko Blue' most reliable blue in neutral soil flowering freely into late summer; dwarf *H. m.* 'Pia', deep red flowers. *Pruning C.* Leave flowerheads on till late spring, then cut back to pair of new leaves.

ILEX (holly) You might consider it a tree in the South, but holly is invaluable as a glossy, evergreen shrub. Clip it, or let it grow freeform. If your holly gets too big, just cut it back. Variegated varieties thrive in sun but all hollies tolerate shade. If you have growing space for just one holly, choose a self-fertile one – i.e., one that doesn't need a mate to produce berries.

Best Bets: I. x *meserveae* 'Blue Princess' and 'Blue Stallion', dark green, rounded leaves and scarlet berries; *I.* 'China Boy' and 'China Girl', 6ft (1.8m) tall and 8-10ft (2.5-3m) spread. *Pruning C.* Unless training to shape.

JASMINUM NUDIFLORUM (winter-flowering jasmine) In warmer parts of the country, this deciduous shrub provides dainty yellow star flowers along its leafless stems in winter. Fine on a shady wall, but best in full sun. Reaches 10ft (3m) high and as wide. Leave the floppy branches to trail untidily but charmingly, or persuade them to train up trellis. *Pruning A.*

LAVANDULA (lavender) Give lavender a sunny site, sharply drained soil and it will supply those heavenly scented flower spikes in summer above desirable gray foliage. Plant in spring.

Best Bets: English lavenders *L. angustifolia* 'Munstead', mauve; *L. angustifolia* 'Hidcote', rich purple, both 18in (45cm); French lavender *L. stoechas* has tufted heads on squat, gray-green bushes, while *L. stoechas pedunculata* has longer, wispier tufts, pale green foliage, and needs winter protection. *Pruning C.* Never cut into old wood as it won't reshoot.

LAVATERA (tree mallow) Trouble-free and gorgeous, lavatera is a deciduous, quick-growing beauty that flowers right through summer and looks like a multi-branched hollyhock. Prefers sun and best against a wall, or in a corner.

Best Bets: popular variety 'Rosea' has large, sugar pink flowers and reaches 7ft (2m) or more; 'Barnsley' has shell-pink flowers and deeper centers; *L. thuringiaca* 'Ice Cool' is white, small, and needs a sheltered, warm spot. *Pruning B.*

PHILADELPHUS (mock orange) A brief performer in early summer, but what a display! The deciduous foliage is nothing special, but the heavy white blooms and heady fragrance are sensational – and at a time when most other early shrubs are finished. Philadelphus is happy in sun or light shade. Varieties range from 24in (60cm) to 10ft (3m) plus, so choose with care.

Best Bets: P. x *lemoinei* 'Boule d'Argent', with large double flowers; *P.* x *cymosus* 'Conguete', intensely fragrant. *Pruning A.* Cut out about oldest third of flowering shoots.

POTENTILLA A deciduous garden trooper, producing flowers similar to that of a wild rose all through summer, and with no demands except well-drained soil and sun or light shade. Most potentillas barely reach 3ft (90cm). Don't confuse them with their herbaceous relatives, which have soft stems; these are quite wiry.

Best Bets: P. fruticosa hybrids such as 'Dart's Golddigger' which, in flower, appears to be smothered in golden buttercups; *P. f.* 'Sunset', vibrant creamy copper; 'Gibson's Scarlet', bright scarlet. *Pruning B.* Take out old wood in spring.

VIBURNUM This one family of deciduous and evergreen shrubs could keep you in flowers, berries, scent, foliage throughout the year. Viburnums flourish on good soil in sun or light shade. Truth to tell, the trickiest thing about viburnums is deciding which one – ones – you want.

Best Bets: *V.* x *burkwoodii* dark shade-tolerant evergreen with very fragrant waxy white flower sprays in early spring or in winter in more southerly areas; *V.* x *juddii*, 1.2m (4ft), deciduous bushy shrub with fragrant, pink-tinged, white, rounded flowerheads in mid- and late spring; *V. opulus* 'Compactum' (guelder rose), 3ft (90cm), deciduous, rounded bush with white flowerheads in late spring, many clusters of glassy red berries plus red leaves in autumn; *V. opulus* 'Sterile' (snowball bush), 8ft (2.5m), deciduous, globe-shaped flowerheads that start out green and turn white in early summer. *Pruning C.*

SOCIABLE CLIMBERS

The well-dressed garden has vertical action as much to draw the eye upwards as to clothe dreary walls or fences. For extra interest, use climbers with interesting flowers or foliage, like the tricoloured leaves of this striking twiner, *Actinidia kolomikta*.

Climbers add another dimension to your garden. No space for a shrub? Put up a pergola, arch or slab of stout trellis, then plant a climber or three at the base. Convert the utilitarian shed into a flower-covered retreat, give drab garden fencing a layer of leafy luxury, and let clematis scramble up the trunk of a tree and beyond. The time to prune and tidy early-flowering climbers is right after they have flowered, and those that flower later in the year, in early spring the following year.

SUPPORT YOUR CLIMBERS

Before you cover any walls or fences with climbers, it makes sense to cover them first with climber support.

❀ Provide horizontal wires threaded through fasteners (wind vertical wires down horizontal wires to form a large square mesh).

❀ Fix trellis to battens on wall (never attach trellis flush to house wall, close quarters provide disease breeding ground).

ACTINIDIA KOLOMIKTA
Deciduous twining climber, not too vigorous, that can reach 21ft (6.5m) in time. All you need is reasonable garden soil and a sunny fence to display the prettiest leaves in the garden – fresh green, heart-shaped – many of which look like they've been dipped first in white paint, then tipped with pink; in autumn, they finally turn red. In summer, expect small white flowers.

Support System: Horizontal wires. *Pruning:* Take out straggly stems in summer.

HEDERA (ivy) Invaluable family of evergreens, that are unfussy about soil or situation, and can be cut back if they outgrow their welcome. Often slow to establish, so be patient. It's a myth that ivy will harm house walls, so long as they aren't crumbling already, which is when tenacious ivy can get a lethal grip.

Best Bets: Small-leaved up to 12ft (3.6m), *H. helix* 'Goldheart', with yellow-splashed dark green leaves; wavy-edged 'Parsley Crested'. Vigorous, large-leaved

up to 25ft (7.5m), *H. colchica* 'Sulphur Heart', bright green leaves splashed with lime; *H. algeriensis* 'Gloire de Marengo', dark green leaves bordered with white. *Support System:* Self-clinging with pads on aerial roots. *Pruning:* Cut back in spring and summer as necessary.

HYDRANGEA PETIOLARIS (climbing hydrangea) Don't worry if it's slow to start: this lush deciduous climber, with frothy white flowers mid-summer, takes a year or two to get going, then whoosh! It can eventually reach 70ft (20m). Needs rich, moisture-retentive soil, but grows well in shade.

Support System: Self-clinging with aerial roots. *Pruning:* Cut back in spring if it gets too large.

JASMINUM OFFICINALE (summer-flowering jasmine) For southern gardens. Deciduous, up to 40ft (12m). The daintily shaped leaves and clusters

TRELLIS ON WALL

Always provide climbers with a strong support system. Wooden trellis can be a decorative feature in its own right after a climber such as clematis has been cut back. Tie in the stems as they grow.

31

of small white flowers in summer are good enough reasons for growing jasmine against a house wall or over a pergola, but that sensational scent is the clincher. Needs a sunny site.

Best Bets: J. o. affine, with pink-budded, larger flowers; *J. o.* 'Argenteovariegatum', variegated white and green leaves. *Support System:* Stems twine, so good for growing on trellis, but against a wall, tie loosely to wires. *Pruning:* In spring cut out damaged and unwanted stems.

LONICERA (honeysuckle)
Deciduous. This climber is not one for lovers of clipped, neat gardens. Instead, fragrant, free-flowering honeysuckle should be left to romp where it will, as it does rampantly throughout the Northeast and the finest old-fashioned cottage gardens. Just point honeysuckle at the nearest tree or trellis, archway or hedge, and keep it content with good, rich soil and light shade or sun. Red berries in late summer are a bonus.

WIRES AND VINE EYES

Strong horizontal wires, with added vertical wires threaded through eyelet fasteners, form an effective climbing frame that is particularly suited to climbing plants with tendrils, such as fruiting and ornamental vines.

There is no plant that can lend instant cottage garden atmosphere in the appealing, informal way that honeysuckle can, particularly when it is planted as a billowing backdrop to a mass of summer-flowering perennials. This is not a climber that should be trained into submission.

Best Bets: The common honey-suckle, *L. periclymenum*, offers three well-scented good garden varieties all reaching up to 20ft (6m). For early summer, 'Serotina Florida', early Dutch honeysuckle, rich pink coloring; mid-summer to autumn, 'Graham Thomas', large yellow-and-white flowers; late summer to autumn, 'Dropmore Scarlet', long-tubed brilliant red flowers. *Support System:* Tie stems in lightly until the plant is established. *Pruning:* Cut back the oldest third of flowering shoots to ground level each spring.

PARTHENOCISSUS (Virginia creeper) Deciduous. In autumn, no climber looks more stunning on a house wall than the fiery, rich crimson foliage of Virginia creeper. But I do mean house wall; this climber is vigorous as well as tenacious, capable of shinning up to 30ft (9m) plus, in time. All it requires is good fertile soil – and space.

Best Bets: P. tricuspidata, labelled Virginia creeper but more accurately known as Boston ivy, has palm-shaped leaves, and crimson-tinted autumn

colors; *P. henryana* has wonderfully varied, finely cut leaf shape, and silver veins on bronzed foliage that turns brilliant crimson in winter. *Support System:* Self-clinging with adhesive pads, but train until established. Pinching out early on will help broaden coverage. *Pruning:* None, except to cut back unwanted growth in autumn.

VITIS VINIFERA (ornamental vine)
Deciduous. You might relish the prospect of picking grapes from your own garden, but the real point of ornamental vines is the terrific foliage that hits its colourful stride in autumn; grapes are a delicious extra. Plant your vine against a sheltered, sunny wall, fence or pergola – even partly shaded – and it will grow fast.

Best Bets: 'Concord', with large, green vine leaves that turn rich red in autumn, and plump purple grapes that are best for wine and jams. Easy to grow. 'Delaware', with many tiny leaves and small, red grapes with excellent flavor. 'Green Mountain' medium late beautiful white wine grape, dark green leaves in

CLIMBERS AND WALL SHRUBS FOR COOL PLACES

(LITTLE SUN, COLD WINDS)

Clematis alpina, C. macropetala, forsythia, *Hydrangea petiolaris,* ivy, *Jasminum nudiflorum,* pyracantha, *Vitis coignetiae.*

summer. *Support System:* Vines have clinging tendrils, but need to be trained into trellis or wires. *Pruning:* As you're probably not going into commercial fruit production, pruning is simple, just cut back the previous season's growth to one quarter in early spring.

CLEMATIS

Some gardeners are crazy about the large, flat-flowered hybrid clematis, with blooms the size of soup plates, others rave about the daintier species, with their scented spring blossom or delectable hanging lantern flowers. Each has a special charm; the clematis buff is able to choose from a plethora of varieties for flowers year-round. All varieties need similar conditions, a sunny site with good humus-rich soil that is not too heavy or acidic, with shade at the base to keep roots cool. Place a few pieces of broken pot, flagstone or shells on the soil surface around the stem. Keep clematis moist, mulch them in winter, and feed monthly in the growing season with a high-potash liquid feed to encourage them to give their best. (*For imaginative ways with clematis see chapter 8, p. 127.*)

Best Bets: From spring to early summer the smaller-flowered species, ideal for growing through shrubs, start the flowering year. *C. alpina* has nodding lantern flowers ; cultivars include 'Frances Rivis', pale blue, large

flowers. *C. macropetala* has open, semi-double flowers. Next is well-known fragrant *C. montana,* which covers large-scale and is shade-tolerant; cultivars include 'Mayleen', with pink flowers and bronze foliage.

From summer to early autumn the large-flowered hybrids which reach up to 12ft (3.6m), predominate, most flowering early and often repeating later. 'Perle d'Azur', sky-blue; 'The President', purple flowers; 'Nelly Moser', pale pink with deeper pink stripes; 'Jackmanii Superba', rich purple flowers in July. Shorter hybrids such as dark plum 'Niobe', green-and-white 'Miss Bateman' are good for growing in deep containers, and look very decorative supported by a wigwam of canes.

In late summer it is the turn of the vigorous *C. viticella* varieties, with four-petalled nodding flowers ranging from pink to purple. Plant them among shrubs, through climbing roses to complement the flowers or add interest after flowering, even through fruit trees for flower and fruit together! They include dark red 'Mme Julia Correvon',

CLIPPINGS

✄ Use cable clips to secure stems of climbers such as euonymous and ivies. Tape ivy stems to wall with sticking plasters until they take hold and grow in the direction you want.

✄ Protect your eyes from garden canes by placing yoghurt pots, pill bottles etc. over them.

✄ Make cut in wirewool scouring pad and use as collar round base of young climbers to keep slugs at bay.

✄ Flowers of some large-flowered clematis hybrids tend to bleach out in strong sunlight, so are better on walls that don't have direct sun.

and rich violet 'Etoile Violette'.

In late summer and early autumn the distinctive and vigorous *C. orientalis* and *C. tangutica* display their golden lantern flowers followed by silken seedheads; these look wonderful, nodding on high over pergolas; less rampant is *C. tangutica* 'Helios', a compact 5ft (1.5m).

Support System: All clematis cling with their twining leaf stalks, so need adequate support.

Pruning: See chapter 3, p. 59.

Take an amiable host plant such as delectable climbing rose 'Albertine', add a contrasting hybrid clematis that will obligingly clamber through the rose, and you have a doubly appealing display.

33

ROSES OLD, NEW, DISEASE-RESISTANT

The war of the roses, old versus new, presents strong arguments for both sides: the romantic antique shrub roses have blowsy, complex flowers and exquisite fragrance, while the Hybrid Teas offer perfectly formed shapely blooms and a far broader color range.

Decide which camp you are in. For the most part, modern hybrid teas and old roses don't mix well.

THE EXQUISITE OLD ROSE

Their appearance is fleeting, they have an untidy habit and with too much rain, the many-petalled blooms can turn into crumpled hankies, but their sensational beauty and fragrance outweigh the odds. Ravishing oldies include rich crimson 'Charles de Mills', dusky magenta 'William Lobb', white flowered 'Boule de Neige', free-flowering rich pink *gallica officinalis* and relative *gallica* 'Versicolor', which has two-tone pink and crimson stripes.

THE QUITE PERFECT MODERN ROSE

They flower for longer, offer a wide variety of colors and have considerable staying power. Just a few notables among the hundreds available include free-flowering 'Ingrid Bergman' with dark red double blooms, low-growing 'Dainty Bess', silvery-pink flowers with toffee-coloured stamens, white-flowered shrub rose 'Alba Meidiland', soft primrose 'Peaudouce' and large-flowered, sugar pink 'Savoy Hotel'. Good for ground-cover are new disease-resistant, rich pink rose 'Flower Carpet', and 'Hertfordshire', with single carmine flowers, golden stamens.

THE BEAUTIFUL ENGLISH ROSE

These comparatively new roses take the beauty and fragrance of the old rose and mesh it with the wider color range, more compact habit and longer flowering period of the modern roses. Some say they provide the best of both worlds. There are new additions annually but English classics include butter yellow 'Graham Thomas', deep pink 'Gertrude Jekyll', crimson 'L. D. Braithwaite' and apricot 'Abraham Darby'.

THE GARDEN-TAMED WILD ROSE

Species roses are the descendants of all garden roses. Many are too large for the average plot, but there are some sumptuous garden-friendly versions. Outstanding for their vigor, disease-resistance and beauty are the scented *rugosa* roses, perfect for hedging and the cottage garden. They thrive on poor, dry soil. 'Scabrosa' has large shocking pink single flowers and outsize scarlet hips; 'Roserie de l'Haÿ' has wine red flowers and is shade tolerant; 'Blanc Double de Coubert', pure white semi-double flowers, free flowering, shade tolerant. *Rosa virginiana* is a North American native with small cerise flowers and bronze foliage, that makes a good ground-cover.

Healthy and reliable English Rose 'Graham Thomas' combines the best of the old and the new. The fully double fragrant flowers are in the style of the old shrub roses but unlike their ancestors are borne for many weeks over the summer.

There are benefits and drawbacks with both old and new roses. Old roses may not have the lasting power of their more contemporary cousins, but when they are as exquisite and richly scented as *gallica* rose 'Charles de Mills', who cares?

THE DISEASE-RESISTANT ROSE

If you fall in love with a rose, you'll want it, whether it's a martyr to blackspot or not. But there are many gorgeous modern roses that are being bred for disease-resistance, so it's worth looking out for them. Species roses tend to be tough, too. Coppery orange 'Just Joey', lemon and pink 'Peace', silvery pink and apricot 'Silver Jubilee', yellow, shade-tolerant old rose 'Frühlingsgold' are just four with good disease-resistance. Climbers that qualify, include fragrant, shade-tolerant shell-pink 'New Dawn', shade-tolerant, thornless cerise rose 'Zéphirine Drouhin', shade-tolerant 'Mermaid', with bright yellow single flowers, fragrant pink 'Madame Grégoire Staechelin', and cream-flowered shade-tolerant rambler 'Alberic Barbier'.

ATTACHING CLIMBERS

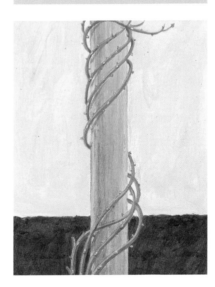

Train the young stems of climbing and rambling roses in a spiral around the support. This will encourage buds to break along the stem, and thus increase the amount of flowers.

THE WELL-BEHAVED CLIMBER...

Check that the climber you choose won't outgrow its space or swamp the garden shed. Beware especially of 'Paul's Himalayan Musk', more at home in its Himalayan habitat than your back garden. More garden-worthy are: shade-tolerant, thornless yellow modern rose 'Golden Showers', snow white 'Climbing Iceberg', pale pink fragrant 'Blairi No 2', pink-tinged, buff-yellow 'Gloire de Dijon' and rich crimson 'Parkdirektor Riggers'.

...AND THE RAVISHING RAMBLER

With many small flowers held in clusters, ramblers flower freely and robustly. A few of the best are: vigorous, fragrant, apricot gold 'Albertine', rich grape double-flowered 'Bleu Magenta', creamy white 'Rambling Rector' and semi-double, repeat-flowering salmon and gold 'Phyllis Bide'.

THE DESIGNERS' DARLING

Often planted in icing-pretty English gardens is 'Little White Pet', an antique dwarf rose with generous trusses of small white pompon flowers. Not an original choice, but a beautiful one.

35

HIGH PERFORMANCE PERENNIALS

Stately Japanese anemones have charming saucer-shaped flowers of white or pink, with a circlet of golden stamens, that brighten the late summer border. Good colonizers even in dry shade, they make an excellent form of flowering ground-cover.

AQUILEGIA (columbine) Start out with two or three planted in sun or semi-shade, and before you know it, you've got a party, in endless, fascinating variations. Spot the seedlings by their rounded, glaucous green leaves on slender stems. In early summer spurred flowers appear in colors of white, pink, purple and blue.

ASTER (Michaelmas daisies) Great for late summer/early autumn flowering, given rich, moisture-retentive soil and a sunny site, but many varieties are prone to mildew.

Best (mildew-free) Bets: A. x *frikartii* 'Mönch', has big mauve daisies, 3ft (90cm); *A. amellus* 'Brilliant' is deep pink, 24in (60cm).

Achillea is an easy-going herbaceous perennial, robust and cheerful. The large flat flowerheads make a bold statement and provide good winter decoration when dried. This variety is 'Coronation Gold'.

These are the plants that will create the fireworks in your garden, and, best news of all, will carry on doing so for years, provided you show them you care with some seasonal attention. All are hardy to zone 4 except where noted.

ACANTHUS SPINOSUS (bear's breeches) From a vast foliage mound arise stems bearing spikes of white and mauve hooded flowers that last weeks in high summer. This 3ft (90cm) architectural plant's needs are few: poor soil, sun or semi-shade, space to stretch out – but it can be invasive. Zone 8-9.

ACHILLEA (yarrow) Good ferny foliage and cheery flat yellow flowerheads make yarrow a good choice for sunny summer borders. Terrific when teamed up with blue and purple plants in the border. If content, it will spread.

Best Bet: *A. filipendulina* 'Gold Plate', bright yellow flowerheads, 3-4ft (90-120cm).

ANEMONE x HYBRIDA (Japanese anemone) Late summer through autumn, daisy flowers are carried elegantly on stiff purplish stems, 3ft (90cm) high, above bold foliage clumps. They'll spread wantonly via underground runners, but can be dug out where not wanted. Will grow equally happily in sun or shade.

CAMPANULA (bellflower) Wide range of valuable cottage-garden perennials, with spikes of bell-shaped flowers in summer, of blue as well as pink and white; perfect with roses. Happy in sun or semi-shade, prefers rich, well-drained soil.

Best Bets: C. lactiflora, branching heads of starry flowers, 4ft (1.2m); *C. glomerata*, chunky spherical flower clusters on 24in (60cm) stems.

DELPHINIUM Fat flower-studded stems in shades from white through blue to purple, beloved by gardeners and slugs. Plant in spring in fertile, well-drained soil, protect slug-susceptible seedlings and stake tall varieties.

Best Bets: Named varieties (including dwarf strains) from Pacific Hybrids or *elatum* groups, *belladonna* varieties have daintier flowers that are spaced more gradually up the stem, 5ft (1.5m) max.

DIANTHUS (pink) Prettiest crimped-edged flowers and blue-gray foliage that thrive given gritty soil and sunshine. For border edges and rockeries.

Best Bets: Lace-edged, fragrant antique varieties such as 'Bath's Pink', pink with crimson center; perpetual-flowering hybrids such as 'Essex Witch', raspberry pink; small carmine-flowered *Dianthus deltoides*.

ERYSIMUM 'BOWLES' MAUVE' (perennial wallflower) A must. For nearly every month of the season this undemanding plant throws out spikes of mauve flowers atop bushy gray foliage; height approximately 24in (60cm). Favors a sunny spot – good grown in a paving gap. With these credentials, small wonder it gets leggy after a few years and needs replacing.

EUPHORBIA CHARACIAS Striking shapes that look at home in every garden and lend green structure as well as immense style. Fat stems of whorled, glaucous evergreen leaves produce giant lime-green flowerheads in the spring; 4ft (1.2m). Grow it in big clumps, even in the smallest of spaces, in sun or semi-shade. Hardy to Washington DC Zone 7.

HEMEROCALLIS (daylily) In late summer, daylilies throw up their tawny-tinted trumpet flowers; they only last for today, but there are plenty more tomorrow. Give them sun or part shade and moisture-retentive soil.

Best Bet: 'Stella de Oro', golden flowers, 20in (50cm), free flowering.

IRIS Large plant family with distinctive flowers and sword-like leaves that grow from a rhizome (thick underground stem), or a bulb. Bearded irises – the beard is the golden, furry tongue at the flower's center – have a broad color and height range: Tall 30in (75cm) plus, midsummer flowering; Intermediate 24in (60cm), early summer flowering; Dwarf 9in (23cm), spring flowering. Plant rhizomes in late summer in sun, exposed, so they get a good baking.

NEPETA (catmint) Strangely scented nepeta makes soft mounds of hazy mauve in the border, and looks terrific *en masse*, as an edging say, for roses. Cats are crazy for it. Best in sun or light shade.

Best Bet: 'Six Hills Giant', 24in (60cm).

RUDBECKIA (black-eyed Susan) Striking daisy of golden petals with a black cone center, flowers from late summer through autumn, given sun or light shade and moisture-retentive soil.

Best Bet: 'Goldsturm', 24in (60cm). A close relative and flowering at the same time is rich pink bronze-centered *Echinacea*.

SEDUM 'Autumn Joy' Drought-tolerant perennial that looks good year-round, providing it has well-drained soil and sun. In spring, it's a fleshy foliage rosette; in summer, stems decked with oval, gray-green leaves are topped with flat heads of pale green buds; by autumn, the pink starry flowers turn bronze, and in winter, add much-needed decoration. Now that's what I call a plant.

Euphorbia characias, with its bold foliage clumps, frothy lime green flowerheads and tough constitution, is an essential plant for all kinds of gardens. Here it makes a sizzling contrast to the bright mauve flowers of honesty, *Lunaria annua*, in late spring.

PERENNIALS THROUGH THE YEAR

SPRING

1 Plant new perennials into prepared soil during mild spells.

2 Protect vulnerable young plants such as delphiniums, lupins from slugs and snails. Watch for late frost.

3 Lift and divide spent and overcrowded perennials *(see Chapter 5, p. 88)*.

4 Tall herbaceous plants can be knocked over by wind if not staked; act before they put on too much growth. Use twiggy sticks such as buddleia and hazel prunings; alternatively, use wide-meshed metal ring suports, on legs, that perennial clumps will grow through and conceal.

5 Lightly fork in general fertilizer around perennials, water in well.

6 Mulch with compost or well-rotted manure; perennials are greedy feeders.

7 Cut back spindly shoots on overwintered tender perennials; start watering and feeding program; move outside when frost danger is passed.

SUMMER

1 Feed with general fertilizer.

2 Step up watering program.

3 Deadhead flowers and flower spikes to promote new flowering growth, and feed for further encouragement.

4 Continue staking.

5 After flowering, lift and replant overcrowded irises and other rhizomous plants. Cut babies from parent plant, and replant with rhizome top above soil level, foliage fan facing sun; snip leaves by half.

6 Keep supporting flower spikes as they grow.

AUTUMN

1 As autumn progresses and the plant finishes flowering, cut back, unless you wish to collect the seeds, or want the plant to self-seed.

2 Leave on flowerheads of sedums, euphorbias, acanthus and other plants that will add ornament to the winter garden, or provide food for birds.

3 Leave stems on Japanese anemones as insurance against a severe winter.

4 Lift and divide overcrowded and spent perennials.

5 Overwinter tender perennials such as windowbox geraniums when they have finished flowering: cut plants back, leaving shoots for spring re-growth, pot each up into pots of compost, water in. Place in frost-free dry greenhouse, cold frame insulated with bubble plastic or on windowsill in cool room.

WINTER

1 If you have stored tender perennials in cold room, insulate window with carpet in very cold weather.

2 Protect crowns of frost-vulnerable plants such as fuchsias with a thick layer of straw secured with chicken wire or bark chippings.

3 Water overwintered perennials very sparingly and do not feed; remove any dead leaves to discourage rotting.

4 Cut back ratty foliage and generally tidy up perennials in the border.

BEST TREES

The simple charm of the winter-flowering cherry is hard to beat, when, in late winter the bare branches are wreathed with delicate flowers in pale pink or white. This small tree looks best against a dark wall or evergreen backdrop.

Out of tiny acorns do mighty oaks grow – and think of the space just one would take up in your garden. Before you decide on a tree or buy it, check out its final size – and unless it's small, don't plant it too near the house or its roots might damage the foundation. A tree should be allowed to develop its natural shape and no regular pruning is needed except to remove the odd damaged or overhanging branch.

ARBUTUS UNEDO (strawberry tree) Is it a shrub? Is it a tree? Who cares, when this delectable, spreading glossy-leaved evergreen with rusty brown, shredding bark produces both white flower clusters and strawberry-like red fruits in late summer. Can reach 20ft (6m) in time. Needs full sun and shelter from strong winds; best in milder gardens.

CERCIS SILIQUASTRUM (Judas tree) Small tree, reaching approximately 15ft (4.5m) in time; perfect for the town garden. Deciduous. Must have sunny, southern site and well-drained soil. Purplish-pink pea-like flowers crowd the branches in late May, then furled leaves open into a heart shape. Red seed pods follow the flowers.

CORYLUS AVELLANA 'CONTORTA' (contorted hazel) A little strange in summer, when less-than-gorgeous curling leaves cover the branches, but worth planting for its leafless months. Those wonderful wiggly branches look highly effective in winter, especially when small catkins dangle from them as spring approaches. Reaches about 10ft (3m) and has a wide spread. Sun or part-shade.

LABURNUM Much loved for the extravagant yellow flower trusses that deck this deciduous tree from late spring, but consider where you position laburnum. Think of the backdrop for all that yellow – green foliage, not red brick wall, please. *L.* x *watereri* 'Vossii' is the garden version that reaches 30ft (9m) in time. Seed pods poisonous.

MALUS 'SUGAR TYME' (flowering crabapple) Good choice crabapple for the small garden, and finest for fruit. Deciduous, up to 25ft (7.5m), with narrow shape maturing to conical. Vibrant green leaves and masses of single white flowers in spring, with a profusion of waxy, orange and crimson fruit, good for jelly, in autumn. Prefers full sun, but will tolerate part-shade.

PRUNUS 'HILLIERI SPIRE' (flowering cherry) One of the finest varieties, preferring, as they all do, a sunny position and fertile, moisture-retentive soil. A cloud of soft pink blossom appears in spring on this broad-topped tree which reaches 25ft (7.5m) in time; new leaves are bronze, then turn dark green before taking on crimson autumnal tints.

PRUNUS x SUBHIRTELLA 'AUTUMNALIS' (autumn-flowering cherry) A tree to fall in love with (I did). In October the bare, twiggy branches display their delicate, frilly white blossoms; 'Autumnalis Rosea' has pale pink blossoms. Plant autumn-flowering cherry by the house, in a sunny spot, and where you can appreciate it from a window; the largest it will grow, in time, is 20ft (6m).

PYRUS SALICIFOLIA 'PENDULA' (willow-leaved pear) See this elegant tree and you'll be hooked. Main selling points are its silver-gray leaves and graceful weeping habit. Cream flowers in spring. Eventually reaches 10ft (3m), and nearly as wide. Prefers sun or part-shade in good, well-drained soil.

ROBINIA PSEUDOACACIA 'FRISIA' (false acacia) Glorious lime-

In late spring *Laburnum* x *watereri* is an arresting sight when the entire tree is dressed in a cascade of bright golden blossoms. Plant laburnum in isolation or as a specimen in a lawn for the full impact of its stunning shape and color.

gold leaves from late spring onwards, this robinia makes a statement which you'll love or hate. The sunny foliage turns greener in summer, then takes on copper tints before it falls. Will grow to 30ft (9m) plus, in time. Drooping white flower clusters from late spring. Not hardy in far north; branches are quite brittle and can break in strong winds.

SALIX CAPREA 'KILMARNOCK' (Kilmarnock willow) No room for that luscious weeping willow? No matter: plant the smaller-scale 'Kilmarnock', a weeper right down to its gray velvet pussy-willow catkins; 10ft (3m)

eventually. When those weeping branches hit the ground, just trim them. Best in rich soil and a sunny position.

SORBUS CASHMIRIANA (mountain ash) Although the large, hanging clusters of pale pink flowers appear in early summer, this deciduous tree is primarily grown, like other sorbus, for its proliferation of berries in late summer; these are an enchanting, pink-tinged white, like porcelain and stay on the tree all winter. Unfussy about situation; grows to 15ft (4.5m) eventually. The fern-like foliage turns red in autumn.

BEST BULBS FOR SPRING AND SUMMER

You can never have too many bulbs (not least because you invariably slice through some of them when making holes for new plants). Few thrills are as great as planting a score or so of flowering bulbs, then seeing them determinedly push their way through the earth – or snow. One essential: well-drained soil that does not become waterlogged. If they're happy, some will settle and multiply. Others are more suited to exhibition bedding.

PLANTING FOR BEST EFFECTS

Plant spring bulbs in clumps under and around deciduous trees and shrubs, among herbaceous plants whose foliage will hide the dying bulbs' leaves later on. Tall hybrid tulips are traditionally planted among flowering annuals in autumn, then lifted to make way for summer bedding. Tulips can be formal, in rows as border edging; daffodils, crocuses and co. are better in natural drifts – scatter bulbs on ground, plant in the positions they fall. Another idea stolen from nature is to plant bulbs in grass, leaving them to naturalize and spread; don't mow until the foliage has died down. Plant spring bulbs and tulips in autumn before the ground freezes.

SPRING-FLOWERING BULBS

GALANTHUS NIVALIS Snowdrops flower first, in late winter. Move them just after they have flowered while the leaves are still green. Give them moist soil, light shade and they'll spread.

CROCUS Plant crocus bulbs in generous clumps to make golden, purple or white pools of early color; if in grass, look for *grandiflora* varieties that can be seen. Best in sun.

Plant bulbs that like the same conditions together for best results. These checkerboard fritillaries look wonderful with dogstooth violets, *Erythronium dens-canis,* because they both grow together naturally in woodland situations.

IRIS Shorter than their rhizomous relatives, spring-flowering iris should be planted where they can be admired, in sunny spots at the front of the border, or in pots near the house. Look for yellow *danfordiae* or violet *reticulata* varieties.

NARCISSI Versatile daffodils make their own splashes of sunshine, even in light shade, and many will naturalize. A host of golden daffodils to choose from, as well as paler tones. Dwarf daffs are great in containers and for the small garden; dying foliage is less obtrusive.

ANEMONE BLANDA Daisy-like lavender-blue windflower, also in rose-pink and white, forms low, leafy clumps with flowers held above. Plant in sunny spots; they will spread.

MUSCARI Grape hyacinth, with their blue floral spikes, look great *en masse*. Plant them in a sunny spot and they'll naturalize. Try two-tone *muscari latifolium*, blackberry and lavender.

SCILLA The well-known variety is the woodland bluebell, but best garden bets are daintier *Scilla siberica* and larger *Hyacinthoides hispanica*. In sun or light shade, they'll spread.

HYACINTHUS The Dutch use hyacinths for annual bedding, but as they invented them, they're entitled. If you leave them in the ground, they'll return next year, a little smaller. Sun or light shade, humus-rich soil.

FRITILLARY Snakeshead fritillary, *F. meleagris,* has a plum and white checkerboard head, and needs moist soil. *F. imperialis*, the Crown imperial, is bigger and bolder, with clusters of yellow, orange or red trumpets. Plant in light shade or sun, in well-drained soil.

TULIPS Grow big, bold hybrid tulips, the last of the spring-flowering bulbs, as showy bedding. Smaller dwarf and species varieties flower from early spring and look good at the front of the border, in rockeries, in small beds.

Best Bets: The choice is vast, and flowering times can vary greatly with each tulip group, so if you want to mix colors together, check their flowering time. Fancier varieties are fringed, lily-flowered, parrot types (cut and frilled petals), and *T. viridiflora* (streaked with green). Of the botanical or species tulips, seek out varieties of *T. pulchella, tarda, kaufmanniana, batalinii.*

SUMMER-FLOWERING BULBS

There are many summer bulbs you can gradually get acquainted with, and all relish sun and well-drained soil. Start by getting to know two of the most glamorous bulb families, alliums and lilies, which look great among roses and other summer-flowering shrubs. Allium foliage tends to die down while the flower is in full force, so plant where leaves can be partly concealed by plant neighbors. Plant alliums in autumn, lilies in autumn or spring and stake tall varieties before they keel over.

ALLIUM Famed plantswoman Rosemary Verey grows thick rows of lilac-flowered *A. aflatunense* under her yellow-flowered laburnum tunnel, and the effect is magical. You can create magical effects in your own garden, too, with these fuzzy-flowered ornamental onions. Chives are one of the humbler, though very pretty varieties, while larger *A. aflatunense* have mauve flowerheads tennis ball size on thick green stalks. *Allium christophii* bears an

Alliums look sensational in mixed borders of shrubs and perennials. To achieve an effect of exuberant abundance, plant these silvery mauve ornamental onions *en masse* and choose varieties of different heights.

GROUND-COVERS

In your garden you need plants that comfortably spread, easing themselves into any broad patch you care to give them, where they will suppress weeds and add their own charm. Many of these listed below will also grow in dark and difficult corners and under trees. In these situations, add lots of compost or well-rotted manure to the soil before planting.

AJUGA REPTANS (bugle) Carpet of small rounded leaves, usually bronze, some forms variegated, from which spring up rich blue tubular flower spikes in early summer. Prefers light shade.

ALCHEMILLA MOLLIS (lady's mantle) Forms clumps of fresh apple-green rounded leaves and foamy lime-green flowers that look wonderful with just about everything. Alchemilla will seed itself all round your garden unless you cut the plant back when the flowers fade.

BERGENIA (elephant's ears) Rounded, large and leathery leaves are vibrant green, then turn red in autumn. In early spring, up come large bluebell-like spikes in white, crimson or pink. Unfussy, best under shrubs or trees.

EUPHORBIA ROBBIAE (spurge) Good-looking evergreen perennial which has refreshing lime-green bracts in spring, and spreads via underground runners. Will grow contentedly in sun

or shade, and in poor soil.

GERANIUM (crane's bill) Invaluable perennials that thrive in sun or shade and any reasonable soil. They form substantial foliage clumps about 24in (60cm) high, flower for months in summer, then disappear in autumn and winter. Many varieties to choose from, in shades of pink, mauve, magenta, blue. 'Johnsons' Blue' has lavender-blue flowers and great vigour; don't be without it.

HEDERA (ivy) Consider ivy not just as a climber, but as good ground-cover for shady, difficult spots, especially under trees and in woodland-type sites. Best for creeping are small-leaved varieties of *Hedera helix*.

HELLEBORUS FOETIDUS (hellebore) The good news about this dramatic evergreen perennial – apart from its clusters of light green, crimson-rimmed cupped flowers in spring – is that it will tolerate dry shade.

VINCA MAJOR/MINOR (periwinkle) Not juvenile delinquents but evergreen spreaders with handsome shiny leaves and lilac flowers; variegated versions add a useful foliage color splash. Use in open woodland. *V. major* about 18in (45cm) tall, *V. minor* a mere 6in (15cm), but never mind the height, watch the width.

outsize head, about the size of a football, of small lilac flowers on a tall, sturdy stem; late-flowering *A. sphaerocephalon* has purple-maroon-shaded small conical heads that start out apple green.

LILIES The first-time gardener's secret weapon! They're exquisite. exotic, yet so easy to grow. Masses of

hybrids to choose from, but fragrant *Lilium regale*, with waxy white trumpet flowers, is outstanding, as is pink, crimson-speckled 'Stargazer'. 'Connecticut King' is splashy yellow; 'Enchantment', a rich flame. *Lilium lancifolium* has speckled orange turkscap lilies straight out of 'Alice Through the Looking Glass'.

HANDS ON

Choosing gorgeous plants and arranging them creatively around the garden is the fancy, fun side of gardening. Carting home a ceanothus covered in dreamy blue blossom and planning to place it right next to that rich pink *Rosa gallica* is sophisticated stuff. But if you'd like the ceanothus to produce masses of blue blossoms the following spring and the rose to flower its heart out every summer, as it was born to do, you'd better learn how to plant them properly. You'll discover that involves more than making a hole in the earth and plopping them in with a prayer and a watering. Plus you'll need to give your plants proper follow-through care, such as watering, feeding, pruning and protecting them, if they are to give back their best, both for the present and in years to come. These basic, easy techniques apply across the board – rather, borders – with few exceptions. After a while you'll find that they become second nature. Learn how to look after your plants and you'll find they'll thrive, rather than merely survive; there's a world of difference between the two.

45

PLANTS AND PROPER PLANTING

Most garden centers these days are so much like convenience supermarkets that the first-time gardener would be forgiven for thinking that proper planting goes something like this: **1** Fall for plant at garden center; **2** Take plant home; **3** Dig hole in earth; **4** Take plant out of pot and plop in hole. To this, you could add a likely step **5** Plant drops dead (or at least looks permanently depressed). Step **6** (even more tragic) First-time gardener throws in the trowel and gives up in disgust. 'What could have gone wrong?' laments the first-time gardener (we'll assume he or she is the persevering type). 'I've watered it, I've fed it, I've talked to it, what more does it want?' The first-time gardener's path to good intentions is, unfortunately, littered with many a stumbling block. A quick post-mortem on the well-trod steps outlined above highlights the potential pitfalls:

1 FALL FOR PLANT AT GARDEN CENTER This is something that has happened to the best of us, and will happen to you, no matter how much I warn you of the consequences. A silver-leaved artemisia winks seductively, and before we can say 'ferny foliage', we're hooked. We simply have to have it, and will work out where to put it later. It's like falling in love with a pair of shoes and buying them when they don't fit. In an already plant-crammed garden, it's like forcing a jigsaw piece into the wrong hole because that's the only hole that's left; we'll squish it in that rather small space somehow. Impulse-buying is a risky business, and garden center cruising often brings its own heartache. The artemisia, which needs a dry sunny site if it's to thrive, puts one big toe in the wet

A luscious shrub like this *Spiraea* x *arguta* will only thrive if given the proper planting conditions. And however much you nurture a plant, it will never prosper if you bought it as a sickly, sub-standard plant in the first place.

CHOOSING A HEALTHY PLANT

When you buy a plant from the garden center, make sure it fulfills the basic criteria. A healthy plant has a good root system and lots of healthy leaf growth with promise of plenty more.

However much you want the plant, put it back on the shelf if it doesn't look healthy. Avoid buying plants with potbound roots, spindly growth and leaves that are sparse and yellowing.

clay soil in that shady corner *chez vous*, shudders, and starts its speedy and inevitable downward spiral. Of course, you could be lucky and lose your heart to a plant that will be perfectly at home in the position you choose for it, but the hit-and-miss gardening school is decidedly more miss than hit.

Siting a plant in a suitable spot – considering soil and outlook – is the core of successful gardening. Think of the location before you consider the plant. The credo of famed British plantswoman Beth Chatto, 'Right plant, right place', should be embroidered on our gardening aprons and engraved across our spades. Helpfully, garden center plants are usually tagged with information on the conditions each plant favors, and plant nurseries often give more specialist help. As a useful visual guide, plants that are in their right place look right; imagine cactus growing on the edge of a garden pond for a truly jarring planting notion. There's little point growing a plant in an unsuitable environment, but there isn't a first-time gardener who doesn't think that for them, it will be different... This one will last. It won't.

2 TAKE PLANT HOME Garden centers may stack their shelves high, but that doesn't mean that the quality of the plants is the same down the line. Out of the six viburnums on display, which would you choose to take home with you? Even the first-time gardener knows when a plant looks healthy, but this is one instance where what you see is not always what you get. A good gardener is suspicious. Knock the plant gently out

of its pot, and take a look at the other end (go ahead, for all they know you could be a plant inspector). If the plant appears to be welded to the pot, with matted roots pushing out through the holes in the bottom, put it right back. It's potbound, and as past its sell-by date as an over-the-limit yogurt. You should be staring at a healthy root system that hasn't had to wind itself around and around because it's had

When making a garden, there's little to be gained in fighting nature. These drought-loving plants naturalizing in a stony, sunny plot show the benefits of choosing plants that suit your garden's soil and outlook.

PREPARING HOLE AND PLANT FOR PLANTING

1 Water the plant very thoroughly at least an hour before you are going to plant it.
2 Dig a generously sized hole, and loosen the soil at the bottom with a garden fork. Mix the displaced earth and the loosened soil with soil improver.
3 Check the planting hole is big enough by standing the container in it. If it is too small, always take the trouble to redig the hole until it is twice the width of the pot.

47

nowhere else to go, but is just developed enough to go on rooting in a circle when it's tucked into your home ground. If the plant – sometimes you see field grown perennials for sale like this – appears to have been shoved into the pot, that can stay on the shelf, too. You want a container-grown plant, not a containerized one; there's a world of difference.

CLIPPINGS

✂ Use tights or stockings to tie in climbers or to secure trees and shrubs to stakes; since they're stretchy, they won't rub, or hinder growth.

STAKING A TREE

In a sheltered position, a young tree should need no stake at all. But if the site is windy or exposed, you will need a short stake, about one third of the height of the trunk, that should be attached with special tree ties. This way the tree will be able to move with the wind, and its trunk will grow thicker. To avoid damaging the roots, always bang the stake into the ground before you plant the tree, and remove it a couple of years after planting.

PLANTING

1

2

3

4

5

6

1 Knock the plant out of its pot and tease out the roots. Decide on the plant's best side, and make sure that it faces forward.
2 Set the plant in the planting hole, making sure that the surface of the compost in the pot is level with the soil. Disperse the displaced soil in and around the roots with one hand, holding the plant with the other.
3 Firm the soil around the plant with the heel of your foot.
4 Water the plant very well, so that the soil washes into any remaining air spaces around the roots.
5 Mulch the soil around the plant to a depth of at least 2in (5cm), to conserve moisture and suppress weeds.
6 Make sure that the mulch doesn't lie up against the plant's stem – this could cause the stem to rot.

A healthy plant has a crown (a base) with lots of shoots coming from it, doesn't look 'leggy', i.e. spindly, from straining toward the light, and has lively leaf growth with, on closer inspection, the promise of plenty more. It makes sense to see the plant when it's in full growth, but don't choose the one (and it's tempting) that has every flower wide open. Look for a specimen that's in heavy bud, pregnant with blossom or berry. All it needs is to be settled in, and pow! it'll perform its seasonal best in your garden, not on the garden-center shelf.

❀ A word about buying big, big specimens: don't. An increasing number of garden centers and nurseries are stocking larger and therefore mature plant specimens for the weekend gardener who likes instant results. The problem with these (predominantly) trees and shrubs, aside from the expense, is they're trickier to plant and don't establish as readily as their

If you have a lot of space to fill, you may be tempted to buy the biggest plant to give instant effect, but in the long run you will be better off planting three young, small plants that will grow together and establish faster.

younger, more adaptable relatives. For an instant large clump – well, nearly instant – buy three of the same shrub (odd numbers always look more natural) and plant them about 2ft (60cm) apart; do the same, on a smaller scale, with smaller plants. Eventually they'll merge together and appear to be one.

3 DIG HOLE IN EARTH This seems straightforward, provided you don't adopt the popular (for popular, read lazy) approach of digging a hole and making it a neat little planting pocket. Many first-time gardeners are told to line the hole with peat, as a sort of welcoming gesture for the plant, so that the real earth isn't too much of a shock to a plant brought up on planting compost. They then hurl in all sorts of good things – bonemeal, minerals, manure, you name it – just like the ancient Egyptians who buried their kings with everything they'd need to live on throughout eternity. The surrounding soil isn't touched, but the garden is full of these powerhouse pockets, each containing a pampered (and frequently overfed) plant. The theory seems sound but the practice is less so. Heavy, unworked soil stays impenetrable outside the planting pocket so roots can't penetrate; while an excess of gourmet food finishes the plant off.

DON'T GIVE UP ON A PLANT

One of the most heartening experiences in gardening – there are many – is watching plants seemingly come back from the dead to thrive again. Initially, the first-time gardener can't get over how the bunch of twigs in mid-winter leaps into life in spring, all bustling bud and fresh green leaf. But care is needed to ensure that plants which seem sickly or refuse to grow at all are not dug up and consigned to the compost heap before their time. Clematis is a classic. Those thin, weedy stems couldn't possibly produce anything ever again – but they do. Plants also take time to establish themselves, sometimes sitting there for a season or three before suddenly shooting up in great spurts. Others deeply resent being transplanted – ceanothus and holly, for example – but although they may not survive the move, there's also a chance they'll eventually rally. In other words, be patient: never pull out a plant until you have given it every chance to prove you wrong. I once planted a large container-grown holly and watched while most of the leaves turned brown and droped off to form a prickly mulch beneath. 'It will never survive,' said a landscape gardener when he saw the damage. I watched, I waited, I watered. Six months later, my holly is thriving, and has already produced a decent crop of berries.

49

REPLANT DISEASE

You've just moved to a new garden and want to replace the tangerine Hybrid Tea with a prettier pastel pink rose. Don't plant the new one on the same site, because, unless you change the earth to a depth of at least 18in (45cm), the new rose will never thrive in that same spot. Instead, plant it further along, and save yourself the heartache (and the backache). Different plants take up different nutrients from the soil, leaving it depleted; they can also leave disease for the next plant from the same family to pick up. Roses, as well as some vegetables and fruit trees, are the worst affected by this syndrome. So it's wise to play safe and avoid planting any plants in the same spot, unless you put at least a year between them.

Plants don't conveniently stay in circular pockets; they have questing roots, so the soil should be in good condition right across the board, or rather, the garden. All that you need is a spadeful or two of soil improver such as home-made compost or composted bark forked into the soil at the base of the hole and the displaced earth, and a little slow-release fertilizer (*see Feeds and Fertilizers, p. 55*). The other danger is that the planting hole is too small, and the roots are fitted into it; it's preferable for the hole to fit the roots! The hole must be big enough – digging is good exercise, after all – to accommodate comfortably the spread-out roots, so it needs to be at least twice the width of the pot.

4 TAKE PLANT OUT OF POT AND PLOP IN HOLE Hate to make you nervous, but this one can be a killer, literally. First potentially fatal move is putting dried-out plant into freshly watered hole. Right move, of course, is to thoroughly water plant well before planting, giving it time to soak through. Second danger move is to pop the plant into the hole as it comes out of the pot. You must at least partly tease out the roots of a new plant – give it that gently

HEELING IN

Trees, roses and some plants from specialist nurseries frequently arrive bare-rooted, and these need to be settled in to their new homes right away. However, if immediate planting isn't possible, plants should be 'heeled in', i.e. temporarily planted in a narrow trench on a spare patch of earth, and watered in well.

frayed look – so that they reach out into the earth and develop, moving onwards and in this case, downwards. If you don't, those roots will likely twine endlessly and fruitlessly around

PLANTING A CLIMBER AGAINST A WALL

1 First work lots of organic matter into the planting hole to help retain water, as walls absorb moisture. Plant climber at least 18in (45cm) from wall, at an angle so the plant leans towards the wall. Mulch after giving the newly planted climber a thorough soaking. N.B. Plant clematis more deeply than the pot soil level, as indicated, so that it will regrow if clematis wilt strikes.
2 Encourage climbers to cover as broad an area as possible by directing the stems upwards and outwards with canes, loosely attached.

1

2

Planting distances for shrubs

Viburnum tinus

Philadelphus

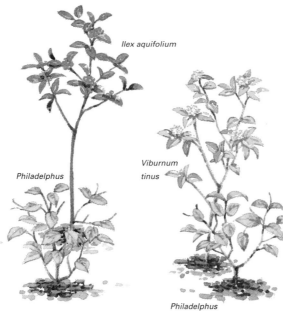

Ilex aquifolium

Philadelphus

Viburnum tinus

Philadelphus

themselves. Post-mortems on dead or sickly plants frequently show that the roots have not budged at all, so that the plant could be neatly popped back in its original pot, even three years later. Third dangerous moment is after planting, when the ground around the plant needs thorough, concentrated watering, not mere social sprinkling. This, by the way, must become a regular commitment, especially during dry periods, until the plant is well established.

WHEN TO PLANT

Traditionally, April and September were the great planting months, but that was when plants were only grown in the ground, not in containers, and sold bare-rooted. Seasonally, early autumn is still the best time for most planting, because the soil is still warm, there is lots of rain, and plants can settle their roots in for the winter before making their spring spurt. They will also be less susceptible to any drought that spring may bring. But provided the soil is workable (not frozen or sodden or baked hard),

container plants can be planted at any time. The exceptions are conifers and evergreens, which should not be planted in late fall unless your garden is sheltered, because biting winds can scorch new young leaf growth. Planting in any extremes of weather, such as during a very dry, hot summer, is courting trouble. Leave any plants that you feel are doubtfully hardy, until spring.

KEEP YOUR DISTANCES!

It's tempting to trek to the garden center and cram an empty bed with shrubs, but if you do this you'll spend the following three years or so weeding them out. By then you'll have grown so attached to that luscious spiraea that you won't be able

to part with it (I speak from bitter experience here). Better to space out the shrubs and either tolerate the gaps – face it, the grandest gardens took time to create, and so will your garden – or fill them with temporary bedfellows such as annuals, bedding plants, and the more compact of the herbaceous perennials.

Plant shrubs too closely together and they'll only compete with one another and suffer in consequence. As a rough guide, smaller shrubs should be planted about 3ft (1m) apart; large shrubs need about 6ft (2m) between them.

P.S. In the first year of planting especially, keep an area of at least 2ft (60cm) around each tree or shrub free from weeds and other plants which will compete for water and nutrients; bark chippings or perforated plastic sheeting concealed with soil will do the job for you.

A spaced-out bed will eventually produce a grand arrangement of mature shrubs.

THE ROSE THROUGHOUT THE YEAR

SPRING

❋ Prune roses in early spring.

❋ Clear away mulch, apply rose feed or general fertilizer. Water well, apply fresh mulch.

❋ Keep newly planted roses well watered during a dry spring.

SUMMER

❋ Spray aphid-prone roses with soft soap insecticide.

❋ Liquid feed after first flowering.

❋ Deadhead as flowers fade.

❋ Look at roses in gardens to see which you'd like next year.

AUTUMN

❋ Order roses from specialist catalogue.

❋ Clear away summer mulch so that any diseased leaves will be cleared too. Apply fresh mulch to moist soil.

❋ Trim back established roses to avoid wind damage. Tie in new shoots on climbers and ramblers.

WINTER

❋ Hill fallen leaves and soil around base of roses for protection.

A GUIDE TO GROWING ROSES

PLANTING BARE-ROOTED ROSES

❀ Heel in rose if planting is delayed.
❀ Soak rose roots in water for 1 hour before planting.
❀ Dig in well-rotted manure or compost plus handful of blood, fish and bonemeal to planting hole.
❀ Make hole wide enough to house roots comfortably, plus deep enough so that budding union – bulge on stem where rose is grafted to rootstock – is about 1in (2.5cm) below soil level, to reduce risk of suckers.
❀ Shake bush gently as you fill in hole to ensure there are no gaps between roots and soil.
❀ Firm in, water and mulch.
❀ Prune stems to an outward-facing bud, 6in (15cm) from base.

DEADHEADING

Faded flowers detract from fresh, plus rob the plant of energy for new flowering shoots. Cut off faded flower to next leaf joint. When all flowers on a truss have faded, cut whole truss just above second or third leaf formation. Roses that produce hips, such as *rugosas*, should not be deadheaded. Always angle cut away from leaf.

HOW TO BUY ROSES

❀ Bare-rooted, ordered from rose nursery catalogue, for spring planting. *Expect:* snag-free budding union, well-branched root system, with at least two shoots of pencil thickness.
❀ Container-grown from garden center, to plant at any time. *Expect:* firmly anchored plant; strong shoots with lots of new growth; no yellowing foliage or sign of pest or disease. Buy in summer to see rose performing.

HOW TO PRUNE ROSES

Worst thing you can do to roses is not prune them, for fear of doing it wrong; recent pruning trials, using electric hedging shears to hack horizontally at bushes, resulted in as many blooms as traditionally pruned bushes. Moral: there's no mystique to rose pruning, you're merely cutting out old stems and encouraging healthy new ones. The aim: to make a well-shaped, open bush. Always wear thick gardening gloves, and prune to just above an outward-facing bud or 'eye' (looks like a red dot), angling your cut away from the bud.
❀ Prune in early spring, on a mild day.
❀ Start by cutting out all dead wood plus damaged or diseased stems. Cut out weedy stems and any which cross one another.
❀ Cut out congested stems in center to discourage disease.
❀ You should be left with about six key stems that define the shape of your rose bush. For Hybrid Teas, cut back each of these stems by at least half; for other shrub and old-fashioned roses, prune lightly so they don't become top heavy.

SPECIES ROSES Respond to hard pruning if they get out of hand.

HOW TO SPOT A SUCKER

Suckers grow below the budding union since they are shoots from the rootstock. Remove them or they can cause the whole bush to revert. They are easy to identify as they have different leaves and growth habit. Pull them off; cutting encourages them, as does hoeing and forking around the base.

CLIMBERS Need little pruning in first 2-3 years. Cut out oldest stems of established climbers as you tie new ones in. Sideshoots that have flowered should be cut back to 2-3in (5-8cm) in length.

RAMBLERS Most can be left to ramble to their hearts' content. But you'll get the best from them if you thin out old growth to ground level as you tie in new stems.

❀ The pro's trick for producing huge Hybrid Tea blooms? Simply remove the small side buds at the end of each shoot, thereby allowing all energy to channel into the big bud at the center.

53

WATER, THE MOST VALUABLE NUTRIENT

'Why have the magnolia buds dropped off before flowering?' Zillions of distressed first-time gardeners have asked themselves this question. (I did, too, through the tears.) But they rarely come up with the right answer. Because the magnolia wasn't given enough water the summer before. Death by drought is often delayed a season or two, which is why many gardeners look for all kinds of reasons for their plants' premature demise, but never for the watering can or hose. Until they are established – for at least two growing seasons – newly planted trees and shrubs must have regular and plentiful watering. Don't make the mistake of thinking that a newly planted lavender or Russian sage – plants that tolerate dry conditions – won't need watering; they will, during this all-important period of early growth when the root system is becoming established. Always water with intention: shoot for the roots, where the water is most needed, with hose or watering can. Watering frequently but lightly will only harden the soil surface and encourage plants to grow roots near the top of the soil, in an effort to reach the water. Spritzing with a hose in the general direction of beds and borders is equally ineffectual as are sprinklers, for the same reason. To give you an idea of how much water plants need, during a dry spell you can easily empty a 2 gallon (9 litre) watering can (slowly, slowly, through the spout) on just one large plant or one shrub; larger mature shrubs can take twice that amount. Using a rose attachment on your watering can will allow water to better penetrate the soil. The best time to water? At the end of the day, when evaporation is at its lowest.

Rainwater is best for plants, especially if you grow acid-loving plants like azaleas and rhododendrons, when it becomes a necessity. In a water shortage, even bathwater is better than no water (I'm assuming you don't bathe in bleach or similar noxious substance), and won't harm plants. Mulch the soil around a newly planted tree, shrub or plant (*see Chapter 1, p.17*) to help keep moisture in the soil, where it belongs (be sure the soil is well watered first).

RAIN BARREL

Collect rainwater in a barrel which is connected to downpipes from the gutters of the house or greenhouse.

CLIPPINGS

✂ Fasten one foot of a used pair of tights over the drainpipe down-spout to act as a filter, so that leaves and debris are kept from your rain barrel, which should always be covered.

✂ The simplest irrigation system of all: a length of hose with small cuts at regular intervals, laid along the center of a flower bed.

✂ Use barbecue charcoal to keep the water in your rain barrel sweet.

CORRECT WATERING

Make sure water gets to the roots of a thirsty plant such as clematis: pour water directly into a flowerpot or neck of a cut-off plastic bottle buried in the soil alongside.

WATER ALERTS:

❀ How to tell if a plant needs watering/ has had enough water? Check the soil, not the plant: it should feel moist at least 6in (15cm) down from the surface.

❀ Plants by house walls, under trees or by hedges – especially new plants and climbers – need most water of all. The site will be dry, either from the heavy competition or because it lies in a 'rain shadow', which will prevent rainwater reaching the plants.

❀ Sandy soils dry out far more quickly than water-retentive clay soils.

❀ Plants in pots are at greatest risk, particularly in summer, from drying out. Water once daily, twice in very hot, dry weather.

❀ First sign of plant stress through lack of water? Quite simply, and very visibly, the plant wilts; warning signal for fast action.

FEEDS AND FERTILIZERS

HOW YOU CAN KILL WITH KINDNESS

A plant can get fertilizer fatigue; in fact, too much of the stuff can finish off a plant completely. Read the ancient gardening tomes and there's a tonic for all plant ailments, and the first-time gardener is eager to try them all. The temptation to overfeed is overwhelming because surely, if one handful of bonemeal is good, two must be better? Not so. Better is to have humus-rich soil with plenty of nutrients for the plant to take up through its roots; fertilizer, which provides supplementary food for the plant, is second on the list. Too much fertilizer inhibits the plant's uptake of water and plant foods from the soil, and if it touches the plant, fertilizer can scorch. That said, fertilizer used correctly can boost a plant's growth rate, and vigor. Plants have different requirements, but it is impossible for the first-time gardener – or indeed the experienced one – to cater for every diet. Instead of playing plant nutritionist, keep to one general long-term fertilizer for planting, and one quick-uptake liquid feed for when plants are flowering and fruiting. The magic formula for both incorporates the three major plant nutrients in differing proportions: nitrogen (N), phosphates (P) and potash (K). Nitrogen stimulates the greenery (stem and leaf growth), phosphates help root development, and potassium or potash encourages flowering or fruiting.

Organic animal-based blood, fish and bonemeal contains predominantly N and P, the chief nutrients required for promoting healthy growth. Seaweed meal or fish emulsion contains beneficial minerals and trace elements for healthy plant growth, so ideal for the organic gardener is to mix both, and use as one fertilizer. Dehydrated chicken manure, also makes a good general organic fertilizer.

When planting large plants and shrubs, incorporate a small handful of general fertilizer into the soil in and around the planting hole. Smaller plants will be content with less. Greedy feeders – roses, clematis and herbaceous perennials – appreciate a forkful of well-rotted manure worked into the planting soil as well, but don't let roots come into direct contact with manure. Plants from the Mediterranean – think of lavender, rosemary, *Helianthemum* (rock roses), which all grow happily in poor, stony soil – need no feed; free-draining soil is far more important.

QUICK-RESULTS LIQUID FEED

In summer, vegetables, fruiting and flowering plants as well as all bedding benefit from regular liquid fertilizers, especially when their root runs are restricted in containers; plants quickly use up nutrients in limited soil space. Tomato fertilizer is high in potash (the K ratio reads highest on the bottle) and is therefore ideal for boosting flower and fruit development. Dilute liquid comfrey and seaweed extract are both excellent, too, as quick results feeds. If you use a fertilizer with a high ratio of nitrogen (N) on a flowering or fruiting plant, the plant will make lots of soft leaf growth at the expense of flowers.

FOLIAR FEEDS

Plants can take up nutrients through their foliage, not just through their roots. Sickly plants often perk up from a

This young corkscrew hazel benefits from a seasonal scattering of fertilizer.

liquid fertilizer sprayed directly onto the foliage; after a short time it's possible to see wishy-washy leaf color become greener and healthier in hue. Foliar feeds given to healthy plants can also improve disease resistance. They're useful, too, in prolonged spells of dry weather, when feeding through the roots is less effective. You can buy name brands of foliar fertilizer; seaweed extract, rich in trace minerals, is especially effective. Use a pressure sprayer to take the strain off your fingers and tackle many plants with one feed.

SEASONAL SOIL SPECIALS

Trees, shrubs and plants benefit from a seasonal scattering of slow-release powdered or granular fertilizer which will eventually be washed down through the soil. The best time to apply this is at the start of the growing season, in spring. If the ground is dry, water it in well.

55

WHY PRUNE ?

The first-time gardener wields the shiny new clippers cautiously, being as yet uninitiated into the garden ritual of pruning. He is probably wielding the how-to-prune textbook too, which makes the operation tricky before he's begun. Pruning only gets really complicated if you side-step the issue and don't tackle your plants until they've grown lanky and shapeless, by which time you're unlikely to get them back to being neat and bushy again. There's no ritual to pruning or creative talent required, but along with the what-to-chop-when textbook stuff, you do need to understand the principles, so that you can assess each plant individually, and treat it accordingly. After all, would a hairdresser give all of his clients the same crop. The whole point of pruning is to make the plant –

we're talking shrubs and trees – as healthy and productive as possible. Prune properly and you'll get more flowers, more fruit, more green shoots, more vigor. Cutting some shrubs right back to within an inch of their lives seems contrary to this, but once you've cut a *Buddleia davidii* (butterfly bush) down to a couple of buds from the ground, and watched it spring to towering, blooming life in a season, you'll appreciate the sense of it. Deadheading your plants to obtain more flowers works on the same principle, as

does pinching out (snapping off the growing tips of plants with your fingers to encourage fresh growth from beneath, resulting in a bushier plant). Cutting ornamental stems such as *Cornus alba* (dogwood) right down to the ground will produce the brightest coloured bark in the next season. Those gardeners who attempt to keep a large shrub within the bounds of a small space by constantly cutting it back will, in time, discover the basic principle of pruning: the more you cut the plant back, the more it will grow.

PINCHING OUT A YOUNG PLANT

The same principles of pruning apply to young plants as to hardwood shrubs. In order to increase the bushiness and vigour of a young plant, and encourage sideshoots, pinch out the growing tips with your fingers.

Sometimes drastic treatment is needed to bring out the very best in a shrub. The hard pruning of dogwood, for instance, results in plenty of fresh, brightly colored stems the following season.

How much you prune a shrub rather depends on how you want it to look. Keep rosemary unchecked and it will grow big and blowsy; some might consider it charming, but you might prefer it more shapely and compact.

There are other reasons for pruning:
❀ To improve the shape of the plant.
❀ To control the plant's size and spread.
❀ To remove dead, diseased and damaged stems or branches.
❀ To clip evergreen shrubs and hedges into shape.
❀ To clear do-nothing twiggy growth.
❀ To produce a more open, and therefore less disease-susceptible tree or bush.
❀ To prune out foliage that is reverting (e.g. from variegated holly back to plain). Neglect this small job, and the whole plant may revert.

PRUNING POINTERS

❀ Always wear thick gardening gloves; look out for those which have a special thorn-resistant finish.
❀ Have a tetanus shot if you haven't been innoculated in the last five years.
❀ Keep your clippers – and long-handled loppers for thicker stems – sharp; blunt tools can tear and damage.

THE PRINCIPLES OF PRUNING

Take note of the following and you won't go far wrong:

❀ Make pruning cuts just above a bud, sloping away at an angle of 45 degrees; if you angle the cut towards the bud, rainwater can settle and cause rotting.

❀ Keep cuts clean, never ragged.

❀ Cut out weak, dead or diseased stems before you do anything else.

❀ Cut back stems or branches that are rubbing against larger ones.

❀ Prune with the motive of letting air into the center of the plant.

❀ Remove tips of branches of young shrubs to keep the plant dense and bushy, by stimulating growth from lower down.

❀ Remove whole branches of plants back to the main branchwork in order to create a larger, more open plant, by channelling energy into remaining branches.

❀ To encourage plenty of fresh, new growth in mature, tired shrubs, cut back to soil level one-third of the oldest shoots each year.

❀ Cut above outward-facing buds if you want your shrub to spread wide; cut above inward-facing buds if you want it to grow more vertically.

❀ If you're not sure whether it's the right time to prune, check first. You're unlikely to kill a plant by pruning, but you could delay its flowering or fruiting for a year.

❀ Feed trees and shrubs after pruning, especially when you've cut them back hard.

❀ Keep your clippers sharp. For any stems or branches that you can't cut cleanly, use loppers, and for the chunkier branches a pruning saw. But when it comes to major work and branches you can't reach, you should call in a tree surgeon.

SHEARING

Some plants need simple shaping after flowering to keep them from growing too lax. Always clip lavender after it has flowered to remove dead flower stems, but never cut into old wood as it will not regrow.

PRUNING PRACTICAL

Deciduous shrubs that flower in spring and early summer, like this splashy *Kerria japonica*, should have their flowering shoots cut back as soon as flowering has finished, to give them adequate time to produce new shoots for the following year.

SHRUBS AND TREES: WHICH TO PRUNE WHEN

The good news – or the bad news, because pruning is so rewarding that it can turn you into the Hacker from Hell – is that many trees and shrubs need no pruning, apart from removing weak, damaged or diseased branches.

Most evergreens, including conifers, only need an optional summer shape-up with shears (in the spring, if they're summer-flowering). Slow-growing

deciduous shrubs such as hibiscus, azaleas and hydrangeas need little pruning either, and should be allowed to keep their flowerheads all winter; they add much-needed interest, and protect new buds from frost.

The faster-growing deciduous trees and shrubs all need pruning, and these usefully fall into two main groups: first, those that flower in spring and early summer, such as philadelphus, forsythia, kerria, weigela; second, those

PRUNING A SPRING AND EARLY SUMMER FLOWERING PLANT

Follow the above pruning method for all Group A shrubs. Those included in this category are: cytisus, forsythia (shown above), winter-flowering jasmine, kerria, philadelphus, weigela.

PRUNING A SUMMER FLOWERING PLANT

Pruning method for Group B shrubs. Included in this category are: buddleia (shown above), fuchsia, lavatera, potentilla.

58

that flower from early summer onwards, such as buddleia, potentilla and fuchsia. Pruning is very different for these two groups. In the first group, Group A, the flowers are produced on shoots which developed during the previous growing season, so these flowering shoots should be cut back as soon as flowering has finished, to allow new shoots to form. If you prune them in winter or spring, you'll cut off the flowers for that year.

You should prune the second group, Group B, in early spring, before growth starts. Cut back the old wood hard (there is a marked difference between old and new: the old wood is rougher and darker), to a low bud, to encourage vigorous new growth which will bear flowers in the same year. Treat shrubs grown for their colored bark, such as *Cornus alba* (dogwood), in the same way, cutting back hard to promote fresh young shoots with the brightest hues. Group C need no pruning at all except to cut out weak or damaged growth.

CLIMBERS: WHICH TO PRUNE WHEN

Prune and tidy up early flowering climbers right after they have flowered; prune those that flower later in the year early in the following spring. Vigorous growers such as *Hydrangea petiolaris* (the climbing hydrangea) may have to be cut back with shears, right after flowering, to keep them in check. (*See Chapter 2, p. 31-32 for pruning notes on individual climbers.*)

CLEMATIS

Omit pruning those stems carrying delicious dinner-plate flowers at your peril, unless you want a climber with masses of straggly growth, topped by blooms you will need a ladder to see. The key is to know your clematis, which will fall into one of three categories, each needing a different pruning method to maximize on flowers:

1 SPRING- AND EARLY SUMMER-FLOWERING CLEMATIS These include all the small-flowered species clematis such as *C. macropetala* and *C. montana*, which should be pruned immediately after flowering, by clipping the sideshoots back to a few buds of the main framework. These clematis don't need pruning to improve their flower output, but they are such rampant growers that prodigious hacking back with shears may be necessary to keep them from taking over the entire garden.

2 MID-SUMMER AND LATER-FLOWERING CLEMATIS These hybrid (large-flowered) clematis bloom on new shoots, and should be cut back to a pair of fresh green buds about 1ft (30cm) above the ground in early spring. All you need to do subsequently is keep an eye on the new growth and tie it in to the supports.

3 TWICE-FLOWERING CLEMATIS Some clematis flower in summer, and again in autumn. The first crop of flowers are from last year's shoots, while the later crop bloom on the new season's growth. These clematis need less drastic pruning than those of category 2. Simply thin out the stems every year, to keep them tidy and productive, and every other year cut back the oldest stems to 2ft (60cm) above the ground.

A NOTE OF COMFORT: If you still find you get in a terrible tangle when pruning your hybrid clematis, you can always cut the plant back to a fat pair of buds in early spring, and you won't sacrifice flowering wood.

PRUNING A CLEMATIS

1

Prune early flowering clematis by clipping sideshoots back to a few buds of the plant's main framework after flowering.

2

Prune mid-summer and late-flowering clematis by cutting back to a pair of healthy green buds in early spring.

ALL CHANGE!

It is important for the first-time gardener to know how to move plants from one place to the other successfully, because inevitably you will plant too closely and shrubs will soon be nudging one another for bed room. To make an assessment of potential take-outs and transplants, scrutinize the border in late summer, when it is at its fullest, not in winter when there appears to be masses of space.

There is always a risk involved in moving plants, and the larger the plant, the greater the risk of losing it. Garden designers might refer to the garden as the outdoor room, but try rearranging shrubs and plants as you would furniture, and you're in trouble, or

rather, your plants are. If you want to move a plant from one part of the garden to another your aim must always be to cause as little trauma to the plant as possible. A small plant such as an herbaceous perennial or small shrub can be moved comparatively easily by watering thoroughly first, digging it up with as much root as possible, immediately replanting it elsewhere, and watering in well. Do it quickly and it won't even notice. Mature shrubs need more specialized treatment. Move large plants on a dry summer day, and you're putting them at greatest risk. Least stressful transplant time is autumn, after a bout of rain. Enlist a friend's help if the shrub is very large.

CLIPPINGS

✂ When watering in a plant that you have just transplanted, add a little liquid feed to the water so that the plant's roots have help in re-establishing themselves.

PLANTS THAT RESENT BEING MOVED

Transplant the following at your peril, but if you do, and the plants suffer post-moving stress such as foliage fallout, don't consign them to the compost heap prematurely: they could come around. Because these plants don't like being transplanted they are best purchased small. Ceanothus, holly, eucalyptus, *Spartium junceum* (Spanish broom, easy to grow from seed).

FOUR STEPS TO A TRAUMA-FREE TRANSPLANT

1 If the stems or branches are unwieldy, tie them loosely with garden string. Make a wide circle at least 12in (30cm) from the shrub with your spade, and dig a deep trench following the circle's curve. Carefully use your garden fork to loosen the earth around the ball of roots, and then gently fork excess earth from around the roots.

2 Dig your spade under the rootball as far as you can, levering gently. Aim to loosen the shrub from the soil with as large a rootball attached to it as possible, but you may find that you have to sever some roots in the process.

3 When you feel the shrub move, tilt it to one side and slide a length of burlap or plastic sheeting under the rootball. Tilt the shrub the other way and pull the burlap through from underneath. Wrap the burlap around the rootball and tie securely; this prevents water loss and keeps rootball and soil intact.

4 Lift the shrub from the planting hole and move to new prepared planting hole, which should have a slow-release fertilizer and organic matter forked into the soil. Unwrap burlap and carefully position shrub to its original depth. Fill in with displaced soil, firming in well. Water in thoroughly and mulch with organic matter.

COVER-UPS

BASIC BEST: THE PLASTIC BOTTLE

Amazing the number of uses a plastic water bottle can have around the garden. With the bottom sliced off and cap removed, it makes an ideal mini-greenhouse to protect a cherished seedling from slugs and pests, fierce winds and early frost. That warmer, greenhouse atmosphere will also help the plant to grow quickly and sturdily. The bottle-cloche will also protect woolly-leaved plants that hate getting excessively wet in spring rains. To make a roomier version, cut a 1 gallon (5-litre) plastic bottle in two, and use both halves, leaving the cap on, but add plenty of ventilation with knife slashes at regular intervals around the sides. Organic gardeners tape several large plastic bottles together to make a box shape that can be dropped around a plant to encourage growth. The bottle-walls are filled with water, not only to act as anchor, but to provide a reservoir of protective warmth. On chilly, plant-threatening nights, the bottles can be filled with hot water, and later on in summer, thirsty vegetables can be drop-fed by making a small hole near the bottom of each one. For organic, read ingenious.

CLOCHES protect plants from severe weather, speed growth of young plants, prolong the plants' growing season, and warm the earth in spring before sowing. A cloche need be nothing more complicated than two sheets of glass or plastic, secured with clips to form a roof, or the 1 gallon (5-litre) bottle. It can also be a long piece of ridged plastic, secured over metal hoops, a bell-shaped plastic dome, or a rigid small-scale Victorian-style glass house. Cloches will keep winter mud splashes off the snow-white flowers of your *Helleborus niger* (Christmas roses), and will keep the slugs off that lettuce. You'll find them indispensable.

COLD FRAMES are handy for hardening off. What's that? Plants that have been raised indoors can't suddenly be exposed to the outdoors. They need to be subjected gradually to their new environment. That doesn't mean you need to shift them indoors and outdoors at the speed of light. When they're seedlings or baby plants, place them in the cold frame and prop open the lid halfway; close it at night. After a week, you can progress to opening the lid wide during the day, and leaving it first a little open, then halfway open at night. After another week or two, consider your plants hardened off.

CROP COVERS These increasingly popular covers, sometimes called floating cloches, are lengths of plastic fabric, tarp or netting that are pulled over crops and pegged down, or pulled over metal hoops to form protective tunnels. The disadvantage is that they're fiddly: on a windy day, try settling plastic tarp over crops without draping it around you. But they will act as a physical barrier to pests, accelerate the growth of young plants, and keep off frost and cold winds, while letting sun and rain through. In severe weather wrap and secure plastic tarp around frost-susceptible plants as well as their containers.

COVERUPS

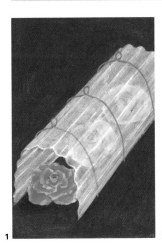

1 A cloche can be as simple as a ridged plastic polytunnel.
2 Let in air – hopefully not pests – by partly raising the base of olde-worlde cloches off the ground with a flattish stone, or twist the top at an angle if it is separate from the base.
3 Cold frames are invaluable for acclimatizing vulnerable young plants to the great outdoors.

1

2

3

HOW TO GROW BULBS

PLANTING DEPTHS

- Ⓐ Crocus
- Ⓑ Grape hyacinth
- Ⓒ Snakeshead fritillary
- Ⓓ Dwarf tulip
- Ⓔ Dwarf daffodil
- Ⓕ Tulip
- Ⓖ Daffodil
- Ⓗ Crown imperial fritillary

3in
6in
8in
10in

Ⓐ　　Ⓑ　　Ⓒ　　Ⓓ　　Ⓔ　　Ⓕ　　Ⓖ　　Ⓗ

HOW TO PLANT A BULB IN GRASS

1 When planting large bulbs in grass, the easiest and cleanest way to remove a plug of turf is with a special bulb planter.
2 To the hole add a little soil mixed with compost and, especially important on heavy soils, some grit to aid drainage.
3 Plant the bulb and replace the plug of turf.

62

DIFFERENT BULB, DIFFERENT DEPTH

As a rough guide, plant all bulbs to a depth of at least twice their height. You cannot plant too deeply, but planting too shallowly can encourage bulbs to divide, and produce more leaves than flowers.

WHEN TO PLANT

Spring-flowering bulbs should be planted in autumn, and settled in well before Christmas so they can put down roots. But you can even plant bulbs after frost, so long as the ground is workable, and they'll catch up. Plant lilies in autumn or the following spring. Settle alliums in the previous autumn.

FEEDING BULBS

Bulbs need moisture while they are growing. If ground is dry, water thoroughly after planting. Daffodils and fritillaries especially need moist soil. Fertilizer is a waste of time when planting, because bulbs have their own food storehouse for the flowers to come, but use a fertilizer after they have flowered.

BUYING BULBS

Choose bulbs that have their shiny coat intact, and avoid those with distortions, cuts, soft tissue or long yellow shoots. Bigger bulbs cost more but flower better; smaller ones may not flower in their first year. Lily bulbs should be fat and fleshy; plant them when you get them, because they should not dry out.

PLANTING BULBS

Dry, loose soils are best because good drainage is vital. Improve heavy, sticky soil by mixing in chipped bark or compost and add grit to planting hole. Either make one big hole for several bulbs, or separate holes for each bulb. Scatter randomly, in odd numbers, to make them look as natural as possible. Twist bulbs when planting into individual holes to ensure they touch the soil. Label bulb planting areas as a reminder.

✿ Planting distances: Large bulbs 4in (10cm) apart; smaller bulbs 3in (7cm) apart; crocuses 2in (5cm) apart.

Aside from a trowel, a special bulb planter is useful for heavy soil, because it removes a complete plug to the required depth. (Useful too for planting solo bulbs in turf.) For planting small bulbs in tough soil, a strong apple corer is useful.

DIVIDE AND MULTIPLY

After a few years, naturalized bulbs crowd one another out, which inhibits flowering. So dig up the clumps after flowering, separate them out, revitalize soil, then replant individually, with wider spacings. Some bulbs are better than others at spreading themselves around. The poet's daffodil, *Narcissus poeticus* is good, as are dwarf daffs 'Tête à Tête', 'Jack Snipe', and 'February Gold'. Species tulips are good naturalizers, but hybrid tulips aren't. In fact, you might find that in their second year, hybrids are smaller. The solution: treat as bedding.

WHAT TO DO WITH BULBS AFTER FLOWERING

Snap off faded flowers to conserve energy. Leave stems and foliage to die down naturally, and don't tie them in knots. Six weeks after flowering, cut them off. Either leave bulbs in ground to flower again, or wait until foliage dies down, then lift bulbs, dry off and store in a cool, dry place until planting time. If you need to remove them pronto to make room for summer bedding, heel them into a spare corner, and when the foliage has dried, lift and store as above.

PLANTING A GROUP OF BULBS IN TURF

To plant a group of miniature bulbs such as crocus, in grass, remove a square of turf from the area to be planted, and plant the bulbs with prepared soil mixed with grit or compost. Replace turf.

DIVIDING OVER-CONGESTED BULBS

Mature bulbs produce offshoots that should be pulled away and replanted. This not only provides you with more bulbs, it prevents bulbs from becoming overcrowded and flowering less.

LAWN CARE THROUGH THE YEAR

SPRING

1 Start mowing when grass starts to grow. Set blades high to inhibit weeds and water loss.

2 Feed lawn; if you use a granular fertilizer, apply with a special distributor and water in well if no rain falls within 48 hours.

3 Brush worm casts, if any, to spread them out before mowing, or the mower will flatten them into a visible lump.

4 Rout out rosette weeds such as dandelion on lawn, and fill gaps with pinch of grass seed.

5 Rake over lawn with a springtine rake to remove thatch, dead grass that mats beneath growing grass.

6 Improve badly draining soil by aerating the lawn; drive a garden fork into the ground all over lawn. Wearing spiked running shoes and walking over the lawn has the same effect!

7 After spiking lawn, brush a mixture of sharp sand and peat into holes to keep them from closing up.

8 Repair bare or damaged patches by replacing with fresh turf, or sowing with appropriate lawn seed. To repair a patch at the edge of the lawn, cut out a square of turf and turn it around so lawn edge is straight and strong. Then sow seed in the worn area on other side.

SUMMER

1 Mow weekly, stepping up to twice a week when neccessary. Don't mow the grass shorter than 1in (2.5cm) high.

2 Trim lawn edges with long-handled shears or scissors.

3 Water lawn regularly, especially in hot weather.

4 Keep on top of weeds in lawn.

5 Feed lawn once more in midsummer.

AUTUMN

1 Mow up till mid-autumn, but allow the grass to grow a little longer between mowing sessions.

2 Rake lawn to remove thatch, dead grass that collects after heavy summer wear, by cutting out each piece with a spade and replacing with fresh turf, or by reseeding area.

3 Improve grass growth by topdressing the lawn; spread a mix of sharp sand, good garden soil and sieved compost over lawn with the back of a rake.

WINTER

1 Rake up fallen leaves, because leaving them to rot on the lawn will kill the grass underneath. Gather them up for leafmold.

2 Don't walk on lawn in icy, muddy conditions, as you will kill the grass; walking on wet grass will compact the ground.

3 Clean and lubricate mower. Store in dry place and cover any parts that might rust.

4 At winter's end, have your mower serviced.

CONTAINER GARDENING

There may not be room for one more plant in the border, but there is always room for one more container. What's more, this particular garden craft is highly addictive. Plant three pansies, and before you know it, you've got a patio packed with pots and no place to sit. Truth is, you can have more fun growing plants in containers than with any other aspect of gardening, and you don't need even green-tinted thumbs to pull it off successfully. You do, however, need creativity and imagination as well as a great deal of potting soil. With container growing you can let your creativity rip, exercise admirable discipline and keep to one color, or allow your gloriously garish streak to flourish. Practically speaking, you can plant in pots the things you can't grow in the ground, like southern camellias or the exotic cactus that snoozes in the living room all winter and spends the summer sunbathing on the patio, flowers blazing. Creative plantswoman Vita Sackville-West believed that you can grow anything in a container, and you know, she was absolutely right.

FIRST CHOOSE YOUR POT

Fritillaria imperialis

There are as many container choices for the imaginative gardener as there are plants to pot. So long as there are drainage holes at the base, you're in business. Before you buy yet another garden-center terracotta flowerpot, open your mind to the possibilities:

❁ Reconstituted stone troughs, or glazed sinks (*see Alpine troughs, p. 73, for how-to-convert*) are terrific for small-scale herb gardens.

❁ Wooden half tubs – but treat with wood preservative.

❁ Old fashioned umbrella stands look good planted up; don't waste soil filling them up. Just wedge a plastic pot in top.

❁ Wooden windowboxes, treated with preservative and lined with perforated plastic sheeting, look rustic left natural;

painted glossy white, they look city-smart.

❁ Brightly colored plastic colanders and ornate wirework baskets make effective on-show hanging baskets.

❁ I've seen giant crown imperial fritillaries (*Fritillaria imperialis*) growing out of a galvanized tin trash can, to great effect. Works best in an urban setting.

❁ Consider lightweight pots for less stress on balcony or rooftop: some terracotta fakes these days fool the eye completely.

❁ Antique copper sink, turned verdigris.

❁ Milk churns.

❁ Paintpots, soup cans and their larger relations, half oil drums – though note that the smaller the container, the more maintenance.

❁ Paint plain terracotta pots in singing Mediterranean shades with strong poster paints, and cluster them together; who cares if it doesn't last? Just paint on another coat next season!

For an instant antique effect paint on milk, yogurt or diluted cow manure to attract lichen and mosses. Tone down spanking new terracotta by painting with solution made from comfrey leaves that have rotted in a plastic bag for several weeks. Another method of mellowing terracotta is by dampening pots and sprinkling them with garden lime.

PACKED POTS: AN EXTRAVAGANZA IN SEVERAL ACTS

Those pansies might be flowering their heads off, but believe me, most of the action is yet to come. For underneath them, layered cosily in compost and

waiting for their moment, are flowering bulbs. A few weeks later the 'Tête à Tête' dwarf daffodils will push their cheery heads up through the pansies. Then carmine-striped leaves will herald the scarlet flowers of 'Red Riding Hood' tulips. But the most spectacular effect is saved for summer when fragrant, sensational lilies will shoot up like rockets through the petunias. Packing a pot with bulbs makes space-saving sense but above all it's amazingly simple and enormous fun. Just when you think the show is over, pow! Up comes another shooting star.

HOW IT'S DONE

Timing: plant in September.

To make a multi-layered pot, you need a deep container of at least 10in (25cm) across, and as broad as possible at base. Arrange plenty of crocks in the bottom, and throw in a handful or two of compost or soil-based compost with a little fertilizer. (This same principle applies to windowboxes, though unless they are especially deep, you'll be limited to just one or two layers; forgo the lilies.) Place three or five lily bulbs on the flat bed of compost, and cover up to their necks with compost. Alternate with tulips on the next layer, then cover with compost. Place dwarf daffodils on top, alternating as before. Store in cold but frost-free place. In spring, top with bedding plants, trying to avoid siting them directly above the daffs (but the bulbs will come through nonetheless; they're persistent).

Watchpoint: Make sure that any bedding plants you choose don't obscure the flowering bulbs. In early spring, for example, pansies will be several inches tall, and will obscure grape hyacinths.

BEST BULBS FOR CONTAINERS

The temptation with a line-up of pots is to plant something different in each, but often it's the simplest arrangements that are the most effective. These grape hyacinths all in a row demonstrate the visual impact of repetition.

Big bulbs in small containers are a flop, in both senses of the word. Instead, choose dwarf daffs and small-scale tulips with bedding plants, although lilies can stand tall.

❀ Lilies are so spectacular that they can be displayed solo in containers. If you want guests to reel at your gardening talents – as well as the heady scent – lilies will do it every time. Pot up in compost either in autumn and store in a cold, frost free place, or the following spring for slightly later flowers. Keep the compost just moist and pull the pot into view when the green shoots come up. Choose from classic *Lilium regale* (the gloriously fragrant, waxy-white lilies streaked with pink), speckled orange tiger lily (*L. lancifolium*), or any of the colourful hybrids. Stake as necessary. Outstanding crimson 'Star Gazer' and rich orange 'Enchantment' are more compact growers well suited to pots. Change compost every other year.

❀ Good dwarf daffs for containers (each of these produces more than one flower per stem): golden-yellow 'Tête à Tête', creamy-lemon, round-flowered 'Minnow', creamy-yellow 'Hawera'. 'Rip van Winkle' has a novel been-through-the-shredder appearance. To give them a cottage garden abundance, plant one snug layer of bulbs in the container, just touching, then offset another layer above.

❀ Good dwarf tulips for containers: scarlet 'Red Riding Hood' with decorative carmine-striped leaves; 'Cape Cod', same leaves, apricot-yellow flowers; vermilion *T. praestans* 'Fusilier' has as many as six pointy-petalled flowers to one bulb, that open wide to the sun.

❀ Tall tulips look good on their own in deep pots, and you can go wild with stripy colours such as red and yellow 'Flaming Parrot', or *T. viridiflora* varieties such as salmon and green 'Artist', without having to worry about color competition from other plants.

❀ Look for beautiful species tulips, too, such as dainty *T. chrysantha*, crimson slashed with lemon.

❀ Blue or white grape hyacinth – use a fine gravel mulch to show these off – look good isolated in pots. For a container 6in (30cm) across, use 12–18 bulbs. Rich purple *Iris reticulata* are showcase bulbs, too: 12–18 bulbs for a 9in (23cm) container.

❀ Dainty bluebell *Scilla siberica* 'Spring Beauty' and the nodding star of Bethlehem (*Ornithogalum nutans)* which has pale green and white bell-shaped flowers, are perfect for naturalizing in pots: you can leave them year after year.

Note: As a rule, don't leave bulbs in containers year in, year out; they never flower as well. Best bet is to plant them in the garden afterwards. The exception is lilies, which can be kept in pots provided you repot them with fresh compost and feed every other year.

PLANTING A MIXED POT

Alternate layers of bulbs in a pot: lilies at the base, then tulips, miniature daffodils or crocus nearest the top. Finally, plant bedding such as early spring-flowering pansies on top.

HOT POTS, HIGH IMPACT

STYLE POINTERS:

❀ Plug plants are great value, but buy them early in the season and either grow them on in the house or coldframe before planting or plant up your hanging basket or container with them, and then grow on indoors, for a head start, until all danger of frost has passed. Otherwise you could end up with dead plants in a sea of compost.

❀ Always gather together more plants than you think you'll need: there are *never* enough. If plants get too crowded, you can always pull out one or two later on.

❀ Big terracotta pots look terrific with just one massed plant. For Mediterranean atmosphere – and evocative fragrance – plant several lavender bushes in one pot; clipped after flowering, they could stay in the pot year-round. In a big strawberry pot, try several kinds of santolina, each with distinctive silvery foliage. Give all the above plenty of grit mixed into the

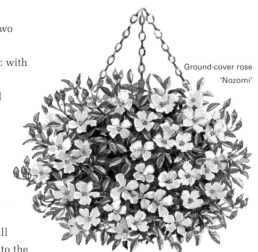

Ground-cover rose 'Nozomi'

WHICH COMPOST

HANGING BASKETS AND WINDOWBOXES A fully planted windowbox or hanging basket can get pretty heavy, especially after watering, so it makes sense to use a lightweight potting soil when planting up. You can find formulations specifically for hanging baskets and windowboxes.

CONTAINERS The weightier soil-based composts help to keep lightweight containers anchored to the ground. Use these for permanent plantings.

For one-season bedders, soilless compost is fine; soil-based and soilless mixed together makes a good balanced container compost that is free-draining, yet retains moisture and is rich in nutrients. Serious gardeners add two garden center ingredients: lightweight perlite and/or vermiculite, which improve soil aeration and drainage, so are particularly good for giving the soil an open texture, which is especially beneficial for cuttings and seedlings.

WHAT IS POTTING SOIL?

Good potting soil is a mixture of compost or humus, peat, sand, vermiculite, perlite or other bulky filler along with lime and nutrients. For seedlings, lighten the mix by adding extra vermiculite, perlite or milled sphagnum moss. Although there are special formulations for cactus and African violets, most potted plants do very well in the soil as it comes out of the bag. Plants in the flowering or fruiting stage may need additional plant food.

Watchpoint: In the last few years many new peat-free composts have been introduced as a response to gardeners who recognize peat as a limited resource and would prefer more ecologically acceptable alternatives. At time of writing the most promising of these is derived from coconut husks, but note that careful watering is needed as well as additional fertilizer: This kind of compost dries out fast.

compost. Classic white marguerite daisies (*Argyranthemum frutescens*) are more temporary, but have an unsurpassed countrified freshness, and look terrific grown as lollipop trees.

❀ Choose the right pelargonium (tender geranium) for the right situation. Upright and spreading pelargoniums are for pots and windowboxes, trailers for hanging baskets.

❀ Roses in containers can look wonderful. Try ground-cover roses in hanging baskets, patio roses in pots. Standouts are frilly 'White Pet', vermilion 'Top Marks' and, at just 18-20in (45-50cm) peppermint-ice 'Green Diamond'. For pure prettiness, grow 3ft (90cm) sugar-pink 'Cécile Brunner' in a glazed blue pot. Small rose bushes need a 12-14in (30-35cm) diameter pot; use a rich potting soil and feed regularly.

❀ Climbers will trail when planted in hanging baskets: black-eyed Susan (*Rudbeckia fulgida* var. *deamii*), yellow-flowered Canary creeper (*Tropaeolum peregrinum*), morning glory (*Ipomoea tricolor* 'Heavenly Blue'), and trailing varieties of nasturtium can all be grown simply from seed.

KILLER COMBOS

SIX KILLER CONTAINER COMBOS FOR POTS OR WINDOWBOXES

❀ *Prettiest silver and pink for spring*
- Peony-flowered sugar-pink 'Angélique' tulips, planted the previous autumn and kept in a cold, frost-free place all winter
- Rich pink, multi-furled ranunculus flowers, overwintered from plugs the previous autumn or bought in bud in spring
- Clumps of silver-leaved *Stachys byzantina* for foliage.

❀ *Purple-plum and apricot for spring*
- A regiment of purple-plum 'Distinction' hyacinths
- Bordering them, a profusion of velvety apricot 'Universal' pansies.

❀ *Cool lemon and lime for summer*
- Splashy creamy-lemon daisy *Osteospermum* 'Buttermilk' or pale yellow *Argyranthemum* 'Jamaica Primrose'

Lemons and golds packed in together, add a brilliant splash of sunshine to the summer garden as in this exuberant planting of golden turks' cap lilies, lemon *Bidens*, primrose *Argyranthemum* and *Helichrysum*.

- Trailing yellow flowers of *Bidens ferulifolia*
- Trailing pale lime foliage of *Helichrysum petiolare* 'Limelight'
- *Lantana camara*, golden flat flower sprays
- Golden marjoram (*Origanum vulgare* 'Aureum').

❀ *Striking bronze and pink for summer*
- Plumes of tall, feathery purple fennel (*Foeniculum vulgare* 'Purpureum'), a fast grower
- *Verbena* 'Royal Purple', trailer with feathery leaves, dainty purple clusters of flowers
- Trailing lobelia (*Pratia pedunculata*) tiny lilac flowers
- Bronze-leaved, pink-flowered *Impatiens* New Guinea hybrid
- Pink geranium with bronze-marked leaves, 'Mrs Quilter'.

❀ *Luscious apricot and blue for summer*
- *Verbena* 'Peaches and Cream', coral, peach and cream
- *Impatiens* 'Salmon Blush'
- *Nasturtium* 'Peach Melba'
- *Ageratum* 'Blue Mink'
- Rich blue *Lobelia erinus* 'Crystal Palace'.

❀ *White, silver and blue for summer*
- *Scaevola aemula* 'Blue Fan'
- Double white geranium 'Hermione'
- *Petunia* 'Ultra Star', white and mauve striped

Verbena, Impatiens, Argyranthemum, Ageratum, Lobelia.

- *Senecio cineraria* 'Silver Dust'
- *Osteospermum plurialis* 'Glistening White', pure white center
- *Convolvulus sabatius*, small trailing cup flowers of lavender-blue.

BEST FLOWERING PLANTS FOR SHADE: Patience plants (*Impatiens*), Small-flowered bedding begonia (*B.* x *carrierei*) pansies, fuchsias, primulas and polyanthus.

LONGEST-FLOWERING PLANTS FOR A SUMMER SHOW: Diascias, penstemons, pot geraniums, verbenas (these pretty, airy plants have another bonus: the flowers die neatly and inconspicuously!)

71

SENSATIONAL HANGING BASKETS

PLANTING A HANGING BASKET

A summer hanging basket presents a terrific opportunity to assemble a mix of tumbling, trailing plants, but do keep to a limited color scheme, as in the rich tapestry of golds and crimsons displayed here.

1 For ease of working, sit basket over a bucket. Line it with an even layer of sphagnum moss that has first been soaked in water; substitute for this is a green mat made from recycled materials, which has a similar appearance, cut to fit.

2 Fill the base of the basket with hanging basket compost or light multi-purpose potting soil, mixed with water-retaining granules, if you wish.

3 Plant the trailing plants first, by gently poking roots through the sides of the basket, making holes in the moss as you go. If you find this difficult, wrap the roots in newspaper and push the newspaper tube through the basket. Add more plants, bearing in mind that they will spread to fill the entire surface.

4 Lastly, plant the top of the basket, adding more soil, placing largest plant(s) in center, and filling spaces with potting soil. Be sure to leave a space at the top of the basket for watering. Water in well. After three weeks, begin a feeding program with a high potash fertilizer.

You need a surprising amount of plants to make a truly gorgeous hanging basket; one champion Chelsea Flower Show exhibitor uses anything up to 48 *Impatiens* to make one patience plant ball! One type of flower such as impatiens, lilac-blue bellflower *Campanula isophylla*, or petunia, can look very effective, but hanging baskets lend themselves particularly well to a selection of trailing plants such as lobelia, verbena, *Lotus berthelotii*, *Felicia amelloides*, ivy-leaved cascading geraniums, *Helichrysum petiolare*, catmint (*Nepeta*), and of course, trailing fuchsias. Use upright, bushy plants in the center, and keep the trailers for around the edges.

CLIPPINGS

✂ To stop summer hanging baskets dripping, water them by putting ice cubes on top of the soil.
✂ Line hanging baskets with conifer clippings to save on moss.
✂ If you have any spare pieces of turf, use them to line hanging baskets, grass-side out; you can trim the grass skirt with scissors!

ALPINE TROUGHS

Alpines – think baby rock gardens – have a small-scale beauty all their own. You can house them in a reconstituted stone trough, or convert an old glazed sink to antique stone trough status, by slapping a gungy mixture onto the surface. Mix equal parts cement, peat, coconut shells, or other bulky organic material and sharp sand into a stiff paste with water. Apply outdoor building adhesive to the sink, and apply this hypertufa with a trowel. You'll need a thick layer of broken crocks or stones in the bottom for drainage. For soil, use a compost-rich commercial potting mix combined with plenty of sharp grit. Raise the trough on bricks so it's nearer admiring

eyes – and to reduce ice damage to roots. Site it in the sun.

Now for the fun: artfully arrange pieces of rock to form the landscape, or use tufa, which many plants will actually root into: gouge out a small hole and prod in the alpine with a little potting soil. Plant miniature spring-flowering bulbs – baby daffodils and crocus. Search out cushion-forming alpines and mat-forming thymes, arabis, saxifrages, houseleeks (*Sempervivum*), rock roses (*Helianthemum*), pinks, sea thrift and blue

Sedum spathulifolium. Top-dress with a ½in (12mm) layer of grit to show off the plants, conserve moisture and prevent them from rotting.

CONTAINERS FOR COLD WEATHER

❀ Thank heaven for spring-flowering pansies which come up with the goods in all but the fiercest weather. Right now, in mid-spring, my windowboxes are packed with a rip-roaring combination of tangerine pansies, carmine-velvet pansies and dwarf scarlet *Tulipa praestans* 'Fusilier'. When selecting pansy colors, bear in

Rosemary, *Solanum capsicastrum, Salvia* 'Purpurascens', *S.* 'Icterina'.

mind that darker colors will have less impact on gray days and cold, windy evenings.

❀ Summer plants spread fast, but early spring plantings won't grow like weeds, so pack them closer in pots.

❀ Ornamental cabbages and frilly kale look terrific in the fall and have a great novelty act: their vanilla, green, and pink shades intensify, when the temperature falls; grow them from seed in late summer, or buy as autumn bedders.

❀ For seasonal berries, choose red-berried barberries, violet-berried 'Beauty Berry' (*Callicarpa japonica*).

❀ A mass of ruby-rich bedding heathers stuffed into a wooden windowbox looks terrific during southern winters; less good, I have discovered, are yellow daffodils peeking through in spring. You could add lollipop topiaries here and there, twisted about with small-leaved dark green ivy.

❀ Innovative British garden designer Dan Pearson favors rich, sumptuous colors, so plant deepest purple black-faced pansies with blue grass *Festuca glauca* and matt black grass *Ophiopogon planiscapus* 'Nigrescens'.

❀ In southern windowboxes where the roots won't freeze, simulate sunshine with golden-leaved evergreen *Euonymus fortunei* 'Emerald 'n' Gold'.

❀ Coloured sages and rosemary work well with orange-berried solanums (winter cherries) underplanted with double white lily tulip bulbs.

❀ Winter hanging basket? Why not? Site it in a sheltered spot – a cool sunroom would be ideal. Try several different kinds of thyme, or delectable trailing willow *Salix repens*, which displays silver catkins in late winter.

❀ Winter-flowering jasmine in a container can be shifted to where it will make the biggest golden splash.

SHRUBS IN CONTAINERS

No space? No problem. For the shrub that you want to grow in the garden but can't find the space for – or the right situation – a large pot can be a long-term solution. There's a bonus, too: for shrubs that have their moment all too briefly, you can pull them into the limelight in a warm bright sunporch at the appropriate moment. In summer give them a break in the garden (but don't forget them, they still need light, water, food) for the rest of the year. Consider the bright pinks of pot azaleas to warm a gray winter's day; big, blowsy *Lavatera* 'Barnsley', decked with palest pink flowers at the height of summer; exotic hibiscus and madcap candy-striped camellias to celebrate spring in a bright sunroom or window greenhouse. Don't worry if you choose a shrub that is destined to hit the sky; the restriction to the roots keeps plants within bounds, and frequently makes shrubs flower more heavily.

SHRUB CONTAINER CARE

Use compost-rich potting mix and a good sprinkling of slow-release fertilizer such as blood, fish and bonemeal mixed in the planting hole. For a small shrub, use a deep pot or tub at least 11in (28cm) across, filled with a deep layer of pebbles or broken pots for drainage; as the shrub grows, gradually increase the pot size without swamping it. Feed flowering shrubs regularly with a high potash fertilizer; foliage shrubs with high nitrogen fertilizer. Prune roots by 2-3in (5-8cm) in autumn or early spring every other year to keep the plant compact, and every spring take off top layer of compost and add fresh, mixed with a sprinkling of blood, fish and bonemeal. Treat with a slow-release fertilizer in autumn, too.

Watchpoint: You may find that after a few years, your potted shrub can't be kept within bounds by pruning, in which case, give it a bigger pot, or a new home.

EDIBLE POT PLANTINGS

Potted vegetable plants can look terrific, but don't expect huge harvests. Especially ornamental are colorful peppers, rich purple eggplants and crimson-stalked ruby Swiss chard. Trailing tomatoes and alpine strawberries can be mixed with ornamentals with great results. Pansies, pot marigolds and nasturtiums, produce spicy petals for colorful summer salads. For fun, grow plants for snipping in a brightly colored plastic colander for colorful summer salads. Suitable contenders are pansies, pot marigolds, nasturtiums (push nasturtium seeds in the compost in early summer).

HERBS IN POTS

Most herbs make fine container subjects. Rosemary, sage and thyme withstand hot, dry conditions, mint is best confined to a container and so is fragrant lemon balm (*Melissa*). Aromatic basil and coriander are compulsory annuals to grow from seed. Scented-leaved pelargoniums, *eau de cologne* mint and pineapple sage are all worthwhile aromatics.

HOW TO GROW

Use a compost-rich potting soil for long-term container herbs, and a lighter multi-purpose potting soil for window-boxes, hanging baskets and annuals. Feed with liquid seaweed when growth starts in spring, and continue through growing period. When picking the leaves, encourage more foliage with regular foliar feeds. Protect from severe weather in winter by wrapping pots and moving plants into a garage, greenhouse or any cold but frost free part of the house.

bay

mint

parsley

thyme

basil

74

CONTAINER CARE

There is no grimmer sight in the garden than a browned-off conifer in a container, non-stop begonias that have stopped, or pansies that simply aren't flowering their little heads off. In the artificial situation of a container, where nutrients and space are limited, great demands are put on plants to perform, so tender loving care is vital. Pack plants into pots, but leave them – especially summer bedders – room to grow. Crock pots at the bottom with plenty of broken pieces of terracotta pots, broken dishes or lots of coarse gravel, use the right compost, and observe the big three: water, feed, deadhead.

WATER

❀ Water once daily in summer, twice on very hot, dry days.

❀ Don't water in freezing weather, because frozen water will make the pot crack.

❀ Do water in bad weather: wind can dry, foliage can cover earth, so no rain gets through to the roots.

❀ Water plants from overhead, using a watering can with a rose; keep watering until the water runs through the drainage holes at the bottom.

❀ If you can't water for a few days in summer, transfer pots and hanging baskets to a shaded position.

❀ If you're not sure whether container plants need watering, stick your finger into the soil: if it is dry 1in (2.5cm) or so down, water.

❀ Water savers: special self-watering containers, and hanging baskets with a water reservoir underneath; a capillary mat allows water to be taken up when needed. Water-retaining crystals mixed into the potting soil when planting help a little.

Pots of tender perennials such as *Felicia, Verbena* and *Pelargonium* make a brilliant summer feature amongst more permanent garden inhabitants. For the best and longest display of flowers, keep container plants well watered and feed and deadhead them regularly.

❀ When planting, don't forget to leave 1in (2.5cm) at the top of the pot for watering.

SMART NOTIONS

❀ Pots sitting directly on their bottoms are in danger of getting sodden so that bulbs rot, plants suffer. Raise them off the ground with bricks or dainty terracotta feet, three to a pot.

❀ Frostproof containers in freezing garages or cold frames, to protect pots and plants, with thick layers of bubble wrap.

FEED

❀ Liquid-feed the foliage, as well as the roots, once-weekly, with the rose on a watering can. Use a soluble or liquid feed; one high in potash such as tomato feed will ensure a good flower show. Underfeed, and the plant won't give its best.

❀ Fertilizer saver: instead of regular liquid or soluble feed, use slow-release spikes pushed into the compost, or granules mixed in when planting.

DEADHEAD

❀ Deadheading – sometimes daily, in summer – not only keeps the display looking good, but encourages more flowers. Snip off (with fingers or scissors) flower and stalk. The more you deadhead, the more will grow! Before going away, deadhead container plants as much as possible; they won't suffer, and you'll have fresh growth to greet you instead of dead flowers.

75

WILDFLOWER CONTAINERS

In a woodland or wildflower garden, potted red geraniums are just too brash. Now many garden centers have a wildflower section, so you can create delectable wildflower container plantings.

❀ In spring, plum *Helleborus orientalis* and checquered snakeshead fritillaries (*Fritillaria meleagris*) of plum, white and palest green look sensational in wooden windowboxes and tubs, especially when mulched with small-scale shredded bark. Buy hellebores in bud as bedding, and plop in potted garden-center fritillaries.

❀ Another spring breeze: sky-blue grape hyacinth (*Muscari armeniacum*) pushing up through variegated periwinkle (*Vinca minor*), with lilac starry flowers, trailing over edges, and maybe some richer mauve aubrietia, looks charming and totally uncontrived.

❀ Baskets have that suitably rustic air. Treat them with a protective coat or three of marine varnish, add a layer of broken-up pots, then line with perforated plastic and treat as a container.

❀ Great wildflower plantings in willow baskets spotted at the Chelsea Flower Show in London, violet and yellow flowers of Johnny jump-up, with ground ivy and native catnip spilling profusely over the edges. For shade, ferns and foxgloves, red campion and bloody crane's bill geranium in a large square willow basket.

❀ For a sunny spot, try a massive potful of furry-leaved, blue-flowered borage, grown simply from seed; to accommodate borage's seeking tap roots, the pot must be deep.

❀ A wildflower nurserywoman created one of the most stunning container

In this wildflower planting, yellow *Lysimachia nummularia*, commonly known as creeping Jenny, combines well with ferns and the wild Johnny jump-up, *Viola tricolor*. Whereas most cultivated container plants prefer full sun, this trio will thrive in a shady spot.

plantings I've ever seen, and what's more, it is suitable for a shady corner: a huge terracotta pot massed with purple-flowered honesty (*Lunaria*) which has the bonus, after flowering, of those opalescent seed pods, dotted with the scarlet and black flowers of pheasant's eye (*Adonis annua*). Her moss-lined hanging basket held a collection of favorite British wildflowers, trailer creeping Jenny, herb Robert, bird's-foot trefoil, wild strawberry, red valerian and daisies. In another pot, she mixed together a happy jumble of corncockle, heartsease, corn marigold and cornflower.

❀ The humble daisy looks pretty in country-style windowboxes, but you could upgrade it to bigger, showier status: *Bellis perennis* 'Pomponette', with red-streaked petals.

❀ Violas lend themselves beautifully to relaxed, cottage garden plantings; for real impact, 'Molly Sanderson' has jet-black flowers with golden centers; 'Huntercombe Purple', midway in size between a pansy and viola, is a rich velvety-purple shade, and has a lemon eye.

FOLIAGE

In a dark, difficult corner of the garden, a big tub of evergreen ferns hides a multitude of murk and makes an exotic corner. From the center of a frothy white alyssum coverlet sprouts an irrepressible cockatoo of matte black grass, *Ophiopogon planiscapus* 'Nigrescens'. Never underestimate the power of foliage in the garden, either on its own, or as a perfect backdrop to display flashier flowers. Some more good choices for containers:

❀ In summer, sprays of silver-gray *Helichrysum petiolare*, with rounded, felty leaves, are indispensable; identical, but colored palest apple-green, is

Ferns and *Digitalis mertonensis*

delectable *H. p.* 'Limelight'. Perfect with geraniums. They look good massed on their own, too, as they have a slightly stiff, spreading habit.

❀ Ground elder might be the scourge of some people's lawns, but buy the variegated version, *Aegopodium podagraria* 'Variegatum', contain in a pot, and you have instant charm.

❀ Bowles' Golden Grass (*Milium effusum* 'Aureum') as it sounds, adds a bright splash of sunshine to the dullest summer's day; use bunches of it in mixed plantings.

❀ A sensational solo shrub: *Acer palmatum* 'Dissectum Atropurpureum' in an oriental-style glazed pot on the patio. As if the filigree, finely serrated leaves aren't enough, in autumn this Japanese maple takes on the fieriest of tints. Is-this-for-real impact: *A. p.* 'Shindeshôjô' has finely laced shocking-pink leaves; cultivar 'Sango-kaku'

(formerly 'Senkaki'), the coral-bark maple, has extraordinary fuchsia bark and lime green lacy leaves.

❀ *Senecio cineraria* 'Silver Dust' is just like a pale silvery-gray lacy doily: tuck in here and there with pastel petunias, pot geraniums, and the like.

❀ Spiky, spidery foliage – garden designers aptly call it architectural foliage – adds a strong, masculine dimension. Cordylines, despite their exotic spear-like leaves, will survive year-round in a southern garden; New Zealand flax (*Phormium tenax*) – full-grown you need serious space – is similarly dramatic, like a Palm Court foliage fan; choose cultivar 'Purpureum' for maroon-purple leaves, 'Variegatum' for stripy green and yellow leaves. Super-spiky *Yucca gloriosa* displays rosettes of deep green leaves from its woody trunk; cultivar 'Variegata' is yellow-striped. As insurance, bring all these semi-tropicals indoors for the winter.

❀ Ivy makes an ideal easy-grow trailing accompaniment to flowering plants in pots, or as a free-fall of foliage at the front of a windowbox. But consider ivy on its own, cascading over a stone urn, say, for an atmospheric evergreen centerpiece. A few highly decorative ivies: bird's-foot rich green *Hedera helix* 'Galaxy' golden-edged 'Goldchild', all-yellow 'Buttercup' (needs sun, or turns lime-green, which isn't bad either), 'Manda's Crested' for burnished winter color.

❀ A big pot of leafy hostas – they're herbaceous, and die down in winter – will thrive in the shade, but protect them against slugs. Particularly good in containers are *H. fortunei* and *H. sieboldii* hybrids; cluster them together with shade-loving ferns and bamboos. Best blue hostas 'Blue Moon' and 'Krossa Regal'.

77

POTS WITH URBAN CHIC

Even the smallest of city gardens can accommodate a surprisingly large number of container plantings. The frequently sheltered conditions and warmer microclimate give city gardeners the opportunity to grow a broad range of plants for most of the year.

echo the moody, urban skyscape of gray skies and stone architecture, as do the gray and silver foliage plants he favors for them. Plantings of thyme and lavender alongside, in slate-shaded windowboxes, simulate cloud drifts on double levels. Ornamental onions, *Alliums*, planted deep in those tin buckets, erupt with showy globe heads of soft mauve, to represent floral puffs of smoke.

🏵 Impatiens thrive in shade and tough conditions that town gardens know all about; keep to smarter single colors, or plant in bands of color, using the flower-filled containers to brighten dull, difficult corners. For cool, city elegance, white can't be beat.

🏵 Simple, striking and low-maintenance: a box hedge in a windowbox. Plant small plants of *Buxus sempervirens* 'Suffruticosa' approximately 4in (10cm) apart, and they will grow into a thick wall of glossy green that you can clip strictly or leave less disciplined.

Watchpoint: Keep all evergreens in tubs, conifers included, well-watered. Allow them to dry out, and they'll take forever to recover, if at all.

THE TOUGH BUNCH

What's the container planting for the ultimate lazy gardener (and the one who doesn't have a plant sitter while he's on vacation)? Cacti and succulents, of course, which look equally good massed in windowboxes, or hanging baskets and sublimely Mediterranean in strawberry pots. If you thought succulents were so-so, try a combination of the silver-blue, swirly rosettes of echeveria (the pink and yellow flower stems are a delight) or

🏵 Sharp, strong colors with evergreen backdrop are the way to go for city-slick windowboxes that are on permanent show. Bright paintbox polyanthus for springtime city pots, and for summer, vibrant geraniums such as lipstick-pink 'Disco', deep cerise 'Barbe Bleu'.

🏵 Standard or pyramid bay trees and clipped box make elegant stand-by sentries for smart town front doors (golden-leaved bay is less common and makes a bigger splash).

🏵 Good reliable evergreen for permanent pot planting is southwest native, Mexican orange blossom (*Choisya ternata*), with an abundance of glossy green leaves and white scented flowers; newer variety 'Aztec Pearl', with similar flowers but with the bonus of fine, spiky leaves.

🏵 A clever garden designer keeps his rooftop plants in deep, galvanized tin flower buckets, their bases punched for drainage; the stacked metal containers

easy-going plummy sempervivums, fir-green trailing sedums like chunky linked bracelets, shiny purple-black tree aeoniums, scarlet-flowered *Kalanchoes* (flaming Katy), day-glo flowered *Lampranthus*, smoky-shaded flowering crassulas ... the variations in colors (from banana to black), in textures and patterns, are quite sensational; to me they're the best-kept container secret.

Plant them in special cactus potting soil and you'll only need to water once every two weeks. As a bonus, some succulents will take root if you simply cut off a piece and prod it into the soil. Gardening was never as simple as this. The resultant foliage or flowering plants will add dash to your container plantings, and will tolerate drought conditions (over a few days: not indefinitely!).

❀ 'Polo' strain of petunias
❀ Potted geraniums can get by on less water than most, but note that the ones you buy from the garden center have been raised in a greenhouse, not a New Mexico hillside, so need more attention if they are to thrive.
❀ *Agave americana* 'Variegata', like a giant spider of yellow-striped green leaves – and after twenty years, you get a flower!
❀ *Cistus* (the papery-fine sun rose)
❀ *Convolvulus cneorum*
❀ Diascia
❀ Gazania
❀ *Helichrysum petiolare*
❀ Lavender
❀ Osteospermum
❀ Sage of all sorts
❀ Santolina
❀ *Sedum spectabile*. More often planted for its use as an indispensable border workhorse, its fleshy foliage somehow takes on exotic status when planted on its own – watch butterflies

flock to the dusty pink flowers.
❀ *Tagetes* (marigold)
❀ Thymes

THE TENDER TOUCH

Geraniums, pansies, petunias, fuchsias, begonias, impatiens and lobelias top the container charts. There is even a new variety of petunia called 'Surfinia' which trails and cascades with almost indecent vigor. But a collection of ravishing tender perennials, only now becoming widely available at garden centers, is threatening to steal the summer show. Some would say they have a subtler, less splashy appeal ... Search out the following, and judge for yourself:

❀ *Bidens ferulifolia* may look delicate, but this yellow-flowered beauty is tough, long-flowering and adds dollops of instant sunshine.
❀ The Swan River daisy (*Brachycome*) boasts swarms of small, sweet-scented flowers in shades from white to purple, with dark centres.
❀ *Convolvulus sabatius*, is a trailing plant from the bindweed family with ravishing lavender-blue flowers.
❀ The kingfisher daisy (*Felicia amelloïdes*) has tiny frothy blue yellow-centered flowers and succulent-like green leaves; those of the cultivar 'Variegata' are lemon-splashed green. The larger-flowered form, with hyacinth-blue flowers and non-variegated leaves, is called 'Santa Anita'. They'll flower throughout winter in a greenhouse.
❀ *Lotus berthelotii* has fine, feathery, silvery-leaved foliage with the bonus of claw-like scarlet or yellow flowers.
❀ *Scaevola aemula* 'Blue Wonder', a comparative newcomer from Western Australia, is a prolific trailer with small lilac and lemon flowers in the shape of a hand.

A TOUCH OF THE EXOTICS

❀ Imagine fizzing 'Jamaican Orange' alongside 'Royal Purple' on your patio: exotic, colourful bougainvilleas, which will grow happily on a sunny patio in summer, and display their papery bracts for weeks on end. Don't overwater, liquid feed and keep them on the dry side in winter, under glass.
❀ Lemon tree very pretty, and if you're lucky it will flower and fruit for you, too. Meyer's lemon has wonderfully scented flowers and leaves, and produces fat, edible lemons. Bring it in to protect from frost.
❀ The novel and numerous baby-blue flowers of *Plumbago auriculata* are a delight, and the plant is, three cheers, relatively pest-free and easy to maintain from year to year. Display in summer outdoors in a sunny, sheltered spot; keep it indoors in winter and cut back in spring.
❀ Away from their more usual setting of city parks' formal bedding, stately cannas – like gladioli gone haywire – come into their own as possibly the most exotic flowers of all, with luxurious strappy foliage sometimes tinted bronze or purple. Dare to cluster pots of the fiery orange, yellow and red shades together. Wow! Keep in pots indoors over winter.
❀ If you can keep off the red spider mite (water-spritz daily), and regularly feed and water the demanding angels' trumpets (*Datura*), a spectacular display of pendulous, tropical trumpet-flowers with a sensational fragrance from summer to autumn can be yours. It's worth the effort. Prune hard after flowering to keep it bushy and keep indoors till next summer.

Watchpoint: Datura is highly poisonous, but only if you nibble it.

79

MULTIPLE CHOICE

If you think that plant propagation – such a long, horticultural sort of word – is too tricky for the amateur likes of you, then consider this: you can get a rose to root by prodding a stem into the ground (all right, there's no guarantee, but that's what keeps you hooked). Plants multiply themselves every way they can, and the encouraging news is you have nearly as much choice in ways of aiding and abetting them. At least one of these methods is certain to fire you with enthusiasm, be it germinating passion flower seeds on the top of the refrigerator, or taking more box cuttings than you'd need to start a knot garden. And plants are so obliging. Bulblets – bulb babies – grow all the way up a tiger lily's stem after flowering, just inviting you to pick them off and plant them for a tiger lily plantation, three years later. And those chunky seeds neatly lined up in sweet pea pods are surely there just for the scooping. Face it, the thrill you experienced at the age of six when growing marigolds in a dixie cup is about to overtake you once more. Don't even try to fight it.

FROM SEED TO HEALTHY PLANT

SOWING AND CUTTING KIT

❧ A dibber. Plastic pencil-like tool (all right, you could use a pencil) is thicker at one end than the other. Use it for making holes in potting soil for cutting or seedling, then easing soil gently around same to make sure there are no air pockets. Slimmer end is also useful for easing out seedling from seed tray.

❧ Rolls of polythene freezer bags in varying sizes, and rubber bands, to make mini- greenhouses for plant babies. A propagator lid or plastic film can be used as a cover for seed trays.

❧ Clippers for taking cuttings from shrubs and plants with thick stems are essential. Use florist's scissors for precise snipping when preparing softwood cuttings. Easier to use than a knife, they have a spring action.

❧ For cuttings, use either seed, cutting or multi-purpose potting soil. Make sure that you have free-draining soil which is vital for cuttings, by mixing 50/50 with sharp sand or vermiculite *(see below)*. For seed sowing, use the same standard seed compost on its own, which you can top with a fine layer of vermiculite.

❧ Vermiculite is a lightweight mineral material that can be used instead of sharp sand because it has a high air and water-holding capacity. It consists of granules of silvery beige spongy material.

❧ Electric propagator, which provides bottom heat to help seedlings germinate and cuttings to root; I get by without this (ever since I cooked seeds to a crisp with one), by germinating seeds on top of the refrigerator, and rooting cuttings on a warm windowsill or in a sunny greenhouse.

❧ Fine-mesh sieve for covering seeds with potting soil.

❧ Houseplant watering can with a fine rose.

❧ Mist sprayer.

❧ Tamper, a block of wood with handle for levelling and firming compost, is surprisingly indispensable. Make your own or use a similar flat object (it's a mystery why you can't buy one).

❧ Plastic pots, mostly 3in (7cm) size; standard, half and quarter-size seed trays. You can also buy plug trays with individual cells for sowing seed and taking cuttings. These are especially useful for sowing large seeds (one per cell).

❧ A cold frame is useful for hardening off young plants and is necessary for housing cuttings and seedlings if you have no greenhouse. Use a brush-on shading wash to protect against direct summer sun.

HOW IT'S DONE

Opening a seed catalogue for the first time is like opening the world on a horticultural Disneyland. So much color, so much choice! And that's only the vegetables. The first-time gardener wants to grow it all: ornamental gourds, citrus-shaded poppies, the entire contents of Monet's Giverny garden in high summer. And you will, but please start out with a few varieties at a time, especially if you have no greenhouse. Otherwise the sunny windowsill (for growing seedlings) could turn into the dining-room table, and the warm refrigerator top (for germinating seeds) could hold many seed trays, little else. And if you're like me, the thrill of seeing fifty seeds of ornamental cabbage germinate before your eyes renders it quite impossible to throw any out. So consider where you'll place fifty pots of cabbages before you sow. I know you'll ignore this advice, because growing from seed is compulsive. And if you plan on growing vegetables, most have to be grown from seed, unless you want to limit yourself to the few boring varieties on sale at the garden center.

❧ You can sow annuals – cottage garden flowers, many vegetables – directly into the ground, and expect good results, provided you have first prepared the soil to the requisite fine tilth (much raking required). Be prepared to thin out overcrowded rows of seedlings as they emerge, and don't over-fertilize the soil if you're growing hardy annual flowers.

❧ You can even fling flower seeds about the place, and many will come up to delight you, but I'm a control freak, preferring to sow in pots and precision plant so it looks, contrarily, as if the seed just landed there in the first place.

🌼 Another option is to sow annuals indoors, keep them in trays until you have chunky seedlings, cut into blocks and plant out each block.

🌼 All seeds need moisture and oxygen for germination. A few also need warmth to get them started. Follow the guidelines on the seed packet for exact conditions.

🌼 Some seeds (often the smallest) germinate in light, but most prefer dark conditions, which means simply covering the seed tray with newspaper; if they're germinating in the warmth of the top of the fridge, they may be in semi-darkness anyway. As soon as the seeds have germinated, remove the covering and put them in the light.

🌼 Seed varies tremendously in size. Chunky seeds like nasturtium can be popped one apiece into cell or plug trays, the plugs of soil later pushed out from beneath; dust-fine seed such as lobelia can be mixed with fine sand and sown in rows from a salt shaker; average-sized seed can be pinched between thumb and forefinger and sprinkled onto the soil, or tapped from

You'll find that both cuttings and seedlings can be grown successfully with the simplest equipment. A range of inexpensive plastic trays and cut-off plastic bottles is all that you need to start your own thriving plant nursery.

the seed packet, as evenly as possible.

🌼 Sow sweet peas several to a deep pot.

🌼 Some seeds that need light to germinate: *Nicotiana*, foxglove,

begonia, impatiens, *Campanula carpatica*.

🌼 Some seeds that need dark to germinate: love-in-a-mist, petunia, sunflower, borage, nasturtium.

SOWING SEEDS IN-SITU

1 To prepare a seed bed for vegetables or annual flowers, first reduce the soil to a fine tilth with a rake. Mark out the plot in a series of sections, one for each variety you are sowing, then draw rows in each section with a stick. Water using a watering can with a fine spray.

2 Sow the seed thinly along the rows.

3 Rake the soil lightly over the seeds and firm down with the back of the rake. Keep the bed well watered and weeded.

83

WHAT GOES WRONG: DAMPING OFF
This fungus occurs in a moist, warm atmosphere. Seedlings flop and are stunted. Move survivors fast, and keep fingers crossed. Avoid damping off by using only fresh potting soil, clean equipment and give seedlings indirect light and adequate air.

WHEN TO SOW SEED

HALF-HARDY ANNUALS Sow these under protection in winter or early spring, then plant out when all danger of frost is past.

HARDY ANNUALS are usually sown in the spring, but for a head start, sow the previous autumn. Sow in a spare patch of ground (protect from slugs and cover with a cloche if in very exposed area) and transfer to final position in early summer, or sow *in situ*. Flowers suitable for this method include pot marigold, fried egg plant, cornflower, love-in-a-mist, clarkia.

PERENNIALS You can sow seed in spring or autumn, but an autumn sowing means that you can have herbaceous perennials in your border, many in flower, by the following summer. For autumn sowings, sow thinly in small pots of potting soil, and leave on a cool windowsill, in a greenhouse or cold frame. When the first leaves appear, grow the seedlings on in 3in (7cm) pots. Keep barely moist to reduce rotting risk and step up watering again in spring. Harden off and plant out in late spring.

BIENNIALS Foxgloves, sweet williams, stocks, honesty, violas, wallflowers should be sown in mid-summer the previous year. Sow thinly in trays or pots, and pot on for chunky plants ready to plant out the following spring. If you want biennials to self-seed in your garden, which most readily do, then you must sow them over two successive years, to get the cycle going.

RAMPANT SELF-SEEDERS

There are some plants that could win awards for reliably seeding themselves in every corner and cranny year after year (leaving you to decide whether they are weeds or welcome). Among them are: candytuft, borage, forget-me-not, cosmos, love-in-a-mist, white alyssum, pot marigold, wild pansy *Viola tricolor*, honesty, aquilegia, *Alchemilla mollis*, red valerian, *Papaver somniferum*, and *Matricaria*, feverfew. If you'd like any of these to be permanent residents in your garden, start sowing, then leave them to it.

HOW TO SOW SEEDS INDOORS

1 Fill tray or pot with compost, and sweep tamping board across tray; tamp down to firm. Water with fine rose sprayer and leave to drain.

2 Sow seed on the surface of the compost.

3 Sieve fine layer of soil on top (depth of layer should equal diameter of seed), or add layer of vermiculite to fine seeds that require light. Cover with plastic film or polythene, and top with newspaper if seeds need dark to germinate. If extra warmth is needed, move to top of the refrigerator, or similar warm place. Check daily for growth, and keep moist, water spraying from above.

4 When first seeds germinate, take off cover and move to good light (not strong sunlight). If indoors, turn daily or seedlings will lean to the light. When seedlings' first true leaves appear, and they're big enough to handle, they are ready to prick out.

SAVE SEED TO SOW

Smart gardeners sow their own seed, leaving a few faded flowerheads on healthy plants so they can collect the seed when the show's over. Late summer, when seed pods turn brown and dry, or brightly colored, is your cue to zip around the garden (yours or someone else's), on a dry day, gathering seed pods.

Watchpoint: Seed of F1 hybrids won't come true to type, so keep to species and old-established hybrids.

Collect in paper bags and bring indoors. You'll need to winnow out the seed from the chaff in the seed capsule. Either the seed will just conveniently shake out of its pod, or you'll need to open up the pod, shake the contents onto a white sheet of paper, and remove the residue. Blow gently to separate the smallest bits of waste from the seeds. If the seed is very fine, you could use a sieve.

Sow right away or place cleaned seed in envelopes or airtight glass jars labelled with plant and date, and store

CLIPPINGS

✂ Cheapest biodegradable pots of all are newspaper pots. Roll up and push in one end for base.
✂ Film canisters make good seed storers.
✂ A circle of newspaper in the base of plastic pots stops soil falling through.

in a cool, dry place until needed.

Easy vegetable seeds to save: peas, runner beans and French beans. Leave them to ripen before taking from plant.

GROWING PLANTS ON SUCCESSFULLY

The essence of succesful home-grown plants is to keep them growing smoothly with as little trauma as possible, so take care when transplanting and never let them dry out.

1 PRICK OUT Move the strongest seedlings to less crowded surroundings so they're at least 1in (2.5cm) apart, either into individual 3in (7cm) pots of soil, or more widely spaced in seed trays. Hold the seedling by a seed leaf, not the stem or true leaf, ease it out of the compost with the dibber, and lower it into a hole made with the dibber, easing it into its new home so that the stem is near buried. Prick out tiny seedlings such as lobelia in small clumps.

2 POT ON When seedlings start to outgrow their limited space, move them again to roomier surroundings so they can develop their root systems without tangling with their neighbors. It's tempting to pot babies on into larger pots than they need, but plants prefer to grow out of pots, not into them, so keep pots on the small side. If repotting into compost-free potting soil, which has a low level of fertilizer, start liquid feeding about six weeks after plant has been in pot.

3 HARDEN OFF Acclimatize pampered indoor-raised plants to the great outdoors with the use of a cold frame or cloche. The way to do this is to gradually increase the amount of ventilation, keeping it closed at first at night, then wedging open a little more every night until the frame is wide open (if frost is forecast, close the frame fast).

4 PLANT OUT Dig a large enough hole, with a trowel, to take the plant's root system, space annuals half their eventual height apart. The base of stem should be level with the soil surface; firm in with your hands.

5 PINCH OUT for bushy plants with masses of flowers. Simply pinch off with finger and thumb the growing tip of young plants when they start to grow vigorously. This encourages fresh growing shoots, and more flowers.

Watchpoint: new buds take time to form, so stop pinching out a couple of months before you want plants to flower.

6 DEADHEAD to ensure the maximum amount of flowers. Don't just take off the flower, but snip or snap off stem, too; removing faded flowers and stalks encourages the plant to focus its energy on producing new flowers.

1

2

85

HOW TO TAKE SUCCESSFUL CUTTINGS

For most shrubs and trees, cuttings are the most straightforward form of propagation.

At its simplest, a cutting is a piece of stem shoved into the soil and left to take root. This works for certain hardy shrubs, but for most plants more finely-tuned techniques are called for. Not all will work. But what do you have to lose by trying?

Here are some general pointers:

❀ Take cuttings only from healthy, vigorous plants, choosing robust young stems. Cuttings root faster when the parent plant is young and healthy.

❀ Take cuttings from non-flowering shoots where possible, so that the shoot's energy is channelled into forming roots, not flower.

❀ Put shoots taken for cuttings in a plastic bag to stop them wilting, and close with a tie.

❀ Always make your cut just below a leaf joint, or node, because much of the plant's growth hormone is gathered at the leaf joint. Severing below that point encourages the cutting to put maximum energy into making roots.

❀ All cuts made should be clean and neat; ragged edges and torn stems encourage disease.

❀ Never take just one cutting, because I can guarantee that it will never root.

❀ Insert cuttings around edge of pot, where drainage is likely to be best, to about one third of their length.

❀ Keep all cuttings moist, using a fine rose on houseplant watering can, as watering is crucial until roots form.

❀ Covering the pot with a fine plastic bag creates a moist greenhouse atmosphere almost like a self-watering system; frequent water misting with a spray is helpful, too. The exception to this keep-moist rule are silvery and gray plants that have coatings on their foliage to protect against water loss and a tendency to rot in damp conditions.

❀ Don't pull up cuttings to see if they've rooted, though I bet you will. A gentle tug will tell if there is root resistance.

❀ As soon as they have rooted, ease them off the self-watering system over several days by making progressively bigger holes in the plastic (if this is being used), then pot up cuttings individually in 3in (7cm) pots of commercial potting soil and harden off.

❀ When to take cuttings? When the opportunity arises. If a gardener offers you a piece of his ravishing cistus, who are you to refuse? Optimum times, though, are given below.

There are three main types of cutting, all of which follow the same principles.

SOFTWOOD CUTTINGS

These are pieces of supple, green stem taken from young shoots. Optimum time for taking these is at the start of the summer growing season, but you can take them throughout summer too. Once the cuttings have rooted, plant them individually into small pots and grow them on until they are sturdy enough to be planted out.

Note: Many softwood cuttings such as fuchsia can be rooted in a jelly glass of water before being potted up.

SOFTWOOD CUTTINGS

1 Choose a vigorous new shoot and cut 3-4in (7-10cm) from the tip, just above a bud. Make a clean cut just below a leaf joint. Snip off the lower leaves to make a clean stem and to cut down water loss from leaves.
2 With a dibber, insert the cuttings around the edge of a small pot filled with fresh potting soil and sand. The leaves should be just above the level of the soil. Water with fine rose spray.
3 Cover with thin plastic and place out of direct sunlight in a cold frame or on a windowsill.

1   2   3

SHRUBS SUITABLE FOR SOFTWOOD CUTTINGS Buddleia, box, ceanothus, ceratostigma, choisya, cistus, cytisus, cotoneaster, escallonia, caryopteris, forsythia, fuchsia, genista, hebe, hibiscus, holly, lavender, perovskia, philadelphus, potentilla, pyracantha, rosemary, santolina, spiraea, viburnum, weigela.

HERBACEOUS PERENNIALS SUITABLE FOR SOFTWOOD CUTTINGS Artemesia, centaurea, diascia, euphorbia, helichrysum, penstemon, sedum.

STEM OR SEMI-RIPE CUTTINGS

These are still young shoots, but they are starting to ripen and turn woody towards the base as summer progresses. Some shrubs will give better results with half-ripe cuttings, but they'll take longer to root. Take cuttings from mid-summer to the beginning of autumn.

SHRUBS SUITABLE FOR SEMI-RIPE CUTTINGS include many of the evergreen and deciduous shrubs listed for softwood cuttings. If you failed earlier in the year with softwood, try again with semi-ripe.

HARDWOOD CUTTINGS

These are longer pieces of stem from hardy deciduous shrubs and trees that are simply pushed into open ground to take root. The nursery site should be sheltered from strong winds and direct sunlight and the soil should be well drained. Take the cuttings in late autumn, just after foliage has fallen. In the case of evergreen cuttings, leave a few leaves on the top.

SHRUBS SUITABLE FOR HARDWOOD CUTTINGS Berberis, blackcurrant, weigela, buddleia, box, cornus, cotoneaster, forsythia, kerria, philadelphus, flowering currant (*Ribes*), rose, willow, spiraea, viburnum.

CLIPPINGS

✂ Save potting soil: put a small pot inside a larger one, fill space between with potting soil and insert cuttings around
.✂ Don't use old potting soil for new plantings; there could be disease present.

STEM OR SEMI-RIPE CUTTINGS

1 Choose sideshoots of the current season's growth, and detach them from the woody parent branch by pulling a small 'heel' from the parent branch.
2 Trim the heel neatly so that there is only a slight thickening in the sideshoot.
3 The prepared cutting should be no longer than 6in (15cm); if it is, cut the tip back to the next leaf node.
4 Snip lower leaves from cutting and continue as for softwood cuttings.

HARDWOOD CUTTINGS

1 Cut a long shoot of current season's growth from the base of the parent plant. Trim just below a bud at the base and just above one at the top; final length should be about 8-10in (20-25cm).
2 Make a deep slit in the ground by working the earth with your spade, and improve drainage with sharp sand.
3 Push cuttings in one by one, 4-6in (10-15cm) apart, leaving just the top 2-3in (5-7cm) exposed. Firm in with your foot. Cover with a cloche or old mayonnaise jar. You should see new shoots the following spring.

87

HOW TO INCREASE PERENNIALS

DIVISION

Dividing and replanting herbaceous perennials every two or three years is a good way to rejuvenate mature plants as well as increase supplies. You'll get clear indications when this satisfying task is needed: clumps become overcrowded, flowers get fewer and often smaller, and some perennials, like sedum, start to collapse from the center. Divide in early autumn (you can see height and spread more easily), or spring (you'll need to water frequently), on a mild day.

Spring, just as the new shoots are appearing, is the best time to divide hostas, after flowering the best for hellebores. Rhizomous plants such as bearded irises should be lifted after summer flowering, and baby rhizomes cut from the parent plant. Replant with rhizome top above soil level, leaf fan facing sun; snip leaves back by half to reduce wind damage.

❧ If you're smart, you can buy a large pot-grown perennial and split it right away to have several for the price of one. Divide with forks or by hand, as shown below, and plant out.

PLANTS SUITABLE FOR DIVISION

Achillea, aster, astilbe, campanula, crocosmia, dicentra, delphinium, echinops, geranium, hellebore, hosta, iris, oriental poppy, phlox, pulmonaria, rudbeckia, sedum, stachys.

ROOT CUTTINGS

Take cuttings of popular perennials with fat, juicy roots in autumn, when plants are dormant. They will be ready for planting out in the following spring. *Note:* Small, thin roots such as those of campanulas and phlox should be cut into 3in (7cm) lengths, placed horizontally on top soil, then covered with top soil.

DIVIDING PERENNIALS

1 Carefully lift out the clump with a spade, and place on a clear piece of ground. If the clump is small and roots fibrous, you can pull the plant into pieces with your hands, taking roots as well as shoots.
2 With bigger clumps, push two garden forks, back to back into the center and prize clumps apart. Plants with thick fleshy roots such as hostas and hellebores can be sliced into sections with a sharp spade or knife, ensuring that there are fresh roots and shoots in each.
3 Discard the center sections and replant the more vigorous outer sections into revitalized soil in groups, or replant in another prepared site. Water well.

TAKING ROOT CUTTINGS OF PERENNIALS

1

2

1 Dig up plant (this is the hard part), and wash excess soil off roots. Cut each root into 3-4in (7-10cm) sections, removing any fibrous pieces and angling lower cut to remind yourself which way up to insert the root. Tops of root cuttings should be flush with soil in pot.
2 Top potting soil with layer of grit, and keep in cold frame. When shoots appear, plant individually into pots of good potting soil, keep them moist and plant out in spring.

PERENNIALS SUITABLE FOR ROOT DIVISION Acanthus, campanula, dicentra, echinops, eryngium, Japanese anemone, oriental poppy, phlox.

TENDER PERENNIALS

This plant category provides some of the choicest summer plants. Why lose them to the first frosts? You can either overwinter them – keep the whole plant through winter – or take softwood cuttings from the plants in late summer, and overwinter those (if you're really organized, you can do both).

OVERWINTERING TENDER PERENNIALS

1 Cut plants back in early autumn, leaving enough shoots for regrowth in the spring. You could use healthy pruned growths for cuttings (see below).
2 Pot each plant up into 6in (15cm) pots of compost and water in well.
3 Place on windowsill in cool room,

frost-free greenhouse (heated preferably), or, in warmer areas, a cold frame insulated with several layers of bubble plastic (cover with carpet in cold weather). Water very sparingly through winter and do not feed.
4 Alternatively, cut tops of plants back hard and store them in fruit boxes of soil, crown of plant just visible. Keep in a spare room or frost-free place, keeping soil almost dry.
5 In spring, cut back any weedy shoots and start watering and feeding program. Move plants outside when danger of frost is passed.

CUTTINGS OF TENDER PERENNIALS
Follow the same procedure as for softwood cuttings, but keep the cuttings in a frost-free greenhouse, heated for preference, a Florida sun room, or on the windowsill of a cool room with good light. *Note:* Impatiens cuttings will quickly root if left in a jar of water, and can then be potted up.

TENDER PERENNIALS SUITABLE FOR SOFTWOOD CUTTINGS Bidens, impatiens, felicia, fuchsia, gazania, osteospermum, verbena.

PELARGONIUM CUTTINGS Pot or bedding geraniums (including the scented-leaved geraniums) need slightly different treatment than other tender perennials but will root easily, even in water, if you like. Take cuttings 3-4in (7-10cm) long, and remove the lower leaves as well as any flower buds and those tiny papery pieces (stipules). Add a layer of sharp sand to the top of the sterile potting soil in a 3in (7cm) pot, and place the cuttings around the edge of the pot. Geraniums are prone to rotting if they are allowed to get too wet, so it's important not to cover the pots, and to water them from beneath by immersing the pot base in water until the soil is moist. Drain thoroughly before replacing on pot saucers. Keep as above; pot up in spring.

HOW TO RAISE YOUR OWN LILIES

Glorious, showy lilies look best in bulk, which works out to a lot of money. Instead, start your own lily nursery. You just need patience, and, of course, a chunky lily bulb or two to start with.

DIVISION As with other bulbs, this is the most obvious way to increase your stock, so long as you have plenty to start with: simply dig up the clump of bulbs after flowering, separate the babies, revitalize the soil, and transplant them. But that's not as much fun as the methods below.

BULBILS You too can have forests of towering tiger lilies, just like those in 'Alice Through the Looking Glass'. It takes time, that's all. Some lilies, notably *Lilium lancifolium*, form

bulbils – miniature bulbs – in leaf axils along their stems, after flowering. Pull these off (don't delay this, because they're there one minute, gone the next) and plant several to a small pot filled with potting soil; they'll produce shoots. Keep in a cold frame or frost-proof shed and the following spring you can plant them out. They'll flower in two to three years. Note: some lily varieties such as the cerise and white stunner *L. speciosum rubrum* produce bulbils underneath soil, next to their roots; follow the same method.

SEED It's true you need patience for this, but if you want spectacular species lilies that would otherwise cost a fortune, what's two years (all right,

sometimes more) waiting time? Sow the seeds in pots or trays and cover them with a fine layer of potting soil. Results from hybrid varieties will be variable, which really means, likely to be inferior.

SCALES Peel off a few outer scales (they tend to be loose, anyway) from just-flowered or bought bulbs in spring or autumn and place them in a plastic bag of moist commercial potting soil. Secure bag and place in warm, dark corner. When bulblets have formed at base of scales, a month or so later, pot them up in potting soil and overwinter in a cold frame or frost-proof shed before planting out the next year. They will take up to three years to flower.

EDIBLES

Lucky you if you have growing space
for a kitchen garden or if you want to be
terribly smart, a potager. Because then
you can grow all manner of fruit,
vegetables and herbs in satisfyingly neat
rows for your own edible, and highly
ornamental, Eden. But even the smallest
plot can find room for a few edible
plants, both everyday and exotic. You
can grow potatoes in a trash can,
summer squash in a container, and
frilly lettuce in the border. And, as I
did, count over one hundred baby
tomatoes on just one plant, artlessly
tumbling from a hanging basket (the
tomatoes, not me). Impress your friends
– and your taste buds – with salads of
peppery arugula, burgundy oakleaf
lettuce, and the sweetest of baby
carrots. Grow culinary herbs as aromatic
shrubs in the border, keeping them
bushy by snipping their fresh young
shoots for the cookpot. Pick juicy
raspberries, blueberries and alpine
strawberries straight from the stem; who
can wait any longer? One word of
warning: be strong at harvest time.
You'll find that home-grown produce
looks (almost) too good to eat.

VEGETABLES

Home-grown vegetables are always fresher and tastier than store-bought. Key to success is to grow varieties suitable for the space you are able to give them. Many vegetables, such as zucchini, will crop happily in containers.

There's no great art to growing vegetables, unless you want monster crops to exhibit in shows (and I can't help you there). So long as you can sow a seed, with a little care you can raise Italian plum tomatoes, Hungarian sweet peppers, French string beans and oriental pak choi. Most vegetables are annuals, so you sow, eat and enjoy, all in the space of months, and, in the case of salad leaves, in a matter of weeks.

SITE AND SOIL

SITE Choose a sunny spot: one that receives direct sun for at least half the day. You can turn a whole patch of ground over to growing vegetables, preparing raised beds with paths alongside; you can grow veggies here and there among the flower borders; or you can use containers – windowboxes and hanging baskets included – for the purpose.

SOIL Start out with weed-free territory, either by meticulously working the plot, or covering with black plastic sheeting and leaving for a season. For first-time veggie cultivation, ideally double dig and leave over winter before spring sowing. Secret of success is rich, fertile soil; incorporate much well-rotted manure and home-grown compost (in subsequent seasons you'll have loads of material from harvested crops). Lighten sticky clay soil with shredded bark. Each year, after the vegetable bed is free of crops, you'll need to incorporate fresh organic matter; you can either dig this in or pile it on top (the no-dig method). Before

sowing, rake in a general fertilizer such as blood, fish and bonemeal, at the rate of 4oz (110g), a couple of handfuls, per sq yd (sq m).

SOWING As a general rule, it's best to sow directly into the soil as long as you're prepared to thin and protect seedlings – beets and other root vegetables should always be grown in this way. Otherwise, sow indoors in pots and plant out when danger of frost is past. (For minimal root disturbance, use biodegradable pots made from rolled newspaper, pushed in at one end for a base.)

GROWING VEGETABLES IN A RAISED BED

A raised bed for growing a selection of vegetables can be as small as 3ft x 6ft (1m x 2m). The big benefits of raised beds: earth warms up faster, drainage is

RAISED BED

For maximum yields, grow vegetables in a raised bed by adding lots of organic matter to the soil. Advantages are that the earth warms up faster, drainage is improved and the plants will mature earlier.

improved, and crops are earlier. How to raise the level of the earth? Easy: all that digging and heaping on of organic matter will make the mound! Edging can be as simple or decorative as you like: a border of bricks; pushed-in planks; flowering chives or marigolds (which will also deter pests plus bring in pollinators and beneficial predators – as will aromatic herbs thyme, sage, rosemary). Use narrow pavers or bricks (grass gets mucky) for walking on and working from, so you never need tread on the beds and ruin your handiwork.

GROWING VEGETABLES IN THE FLOWER BORDER

Plant ornamental and compact vegetable varieties to complement summer annuals and perennials. Tuck in a frilly lettuce, purple-podded dwarf bean, or maybe a cherry bush tomato. Coax trailing squash vines over arches or plant a potato tuber of an early variety to make a lovely leafy mound and give you delicious potatoes when it dies down. Protect from early and late frost with glass cloches. Plastic bottles are not ornamental. Note: a distinct advantage of growing vegetables in the flower border is that they represent a low profile for pests. Massed together, vegetables of one variety are more like a welcoming committee.

GROWING VEGETABLES IN CONTAINERS

Use good commercial potting soil (add vermiculite to lighten hanging baskets) and feed twice-weekly with diluted tomato fertilizer for fruiting crops or fish emulsion for general crops. Be prepared to water once or twice daily in summer; container crops are not low maintenance. For single veg plants, a range of pots 10-12in (25-30cm) in diameter, (plus 6in/15cm pots for one lettuce), is useful. If your containers are

If you want to give early sowings a head start, a layer of horticultural fleece will hasten growth as well as protect the young plants from pests and inclement weather.

on display, grow loose-leaf instead of a here today, gone tomorrow headed lettuce. Have replacements in plastic pots on standby: once you've pulled the finger carrots, with their feathery foliage, there will be spaces to fill. Search out patio and dwarf varieties, sowing in small pots and transplanting into containers when large enough. Try golden bush squash, peppers (chilli and sweet), baby bush cucumbers and eggplant. Choose plants that don't need staking, though several sugar snap peas

or runner beans look pretty in a large tub, shimmying up a cane wigwam. Try quick maturing radishes, finger carrots, salad onions; thin to strongest seedling. Plant trailing tomatoes with parsley in a hanging basket, ruffles of oakleaf lettuce in a windowbox.

GROWING GUIDE

❁ Wait until soil has warmed up before sowing, or crops will sulk. Hasten the process in early spring with cloche, polytunnel or clear plastic sheeting pegged down over site.

❁ Buy pre-treated seed for speedier crops: this has been brought to the point of germination by seed suppliers, so will pop as soon as you sow it.

❁ Look out for seeds of disease-resistant varieties, part of the organic gardener's no-spray strategy for healthy crops.

❁ If you're not sure how deep to sow, reckon on twice the depth of seed.

❁ For final spacings indicator when sowing, think of the finished size of the vegetable, then add a little more space to that.

❁ Hoe between rows of seedlings to prevent weeds taking over the territory; mulching also helps.

❁ Protect early sowings and speed up growth of plants both in the ground and containers, with cloches or blanket.

❁ Always harden off seedlings thoroughly before planting out; any shock to their system, including erratic watering, will check growth.

POTATOES IN A BIN OR BUCKET

Gorgeous it's not, but a big bin planted with just three seed potatoes will provide you with armfuls of potatoes. In spring, plant the chitted potatoes (*see Potatoes, p. 95, for chitting*) 2in (5cm) deep in a half-full bin of potting soil with lots of compost. As the foliage grows, add more compost. Keep frost-free and harvest in summer when foliage fades. Couldn't be easier.

93

THE BEST OF THE BUNCH

This is my streamlined selection; start on these fail-safers and, flushed with success and a wealth of home-grown produce, you can progress to the asparagus bed or kohlrabi plantation. Be brutal about discarding seedlings: you won't need a lettuce grove.

CARROTS My preference is small, sweet varieties to pull in summer.

How to grow: Sow in early spring, covering with cloche, or from the start to the end of summer (thus bypassing the root maggot busy season). Sow very thinly, ½in (12mm) deep, in rows 4in (10cm) apart, or in blocks (as for containers), allowing 1in (2.5cm) in each direction for final spacing. At seedling stage, thin to 1in (2.5cm) apart.

Harvesting: Three-week sowings will give a good supply. Allow at least seven weeks from sowing; carrots should be under 1in (2.5cm) in diameter. Pull or gently fork out in heavy soil.

Best Bets: Finger carrots, 'Short and Sweet', 'Juwarot'; round, 'Kundulus'.

ZUCCHINIS AND SUMMER SQUASHES Scallop-edged patty pan squashes and zucchinis need rich soil, copious watering and high temperatures to germinate. Don't sow till soil is warm, mid-spring at earliest. Choose disease-resistant varieties, and ventilate when under glass. Protect from slugs.

How to grow: For small spaces, choose bush types. For each plant sow three seeds edgeways, 2in (5cm) apart, 1in (2.5cm) deep in 12in (30cm) deep soil pockets enriched with organic matter. If growing several plants allow 24in (60cm) between them. Leave a mound at top and cover to speed things up. Thin to strongest seedling when first two true leaves appear. Keep soil moist around plants – a black plastic mulch

The carrot's biggest enemy is root maggot. Avoid this potential pest by pinching off seedlings at ground level so maggots don't get wind of a potential buffet.

will keep vegetables from spoiling – and feed every 2 weeks when fruits appear.

Harvesting: After about twelve weeks. Cut zucchinis at stem when finger-length. Cutting encourages new fruits.

Best Bets: F1 'Supremo', small courgette, big yield; 'Golden Girl', butter-yellow zucchini, buttery taste, early cropper; 'Defender', resistant to cucumber mosaic virus; 'Custard White', summer patty pan squash.

GARLIC Instead of onions, I prefer to give ground space to garlic: each separate clove makes a large, pink-tinged, aromatic bulb.

How to grow: Plant in late autumn, so garlic develops its root system through winter. Plant each clove pointed end up, the tip just beneath the surface of the soil, 6in (15cm) apart; allow 12in (30cm) between rows. Cloche until warm weather in late spring.

Harvesting: In high summer, when foliage turns yellow, pull a bulb for inspection; it should be 2-3in (5-7cm) in diameter. Clean bulbs, remove stems and hang them in a light, airy place to dry out totally. Store in cool, dark and dry.

Best Bets: Start out with a few healthy bulbs bought from shop or seed merchant, then keep planting from your own stock.

PODS, BEANS AND COBS Peas and beans fix their own nitrogen, so don't need nitrogen-rich fertilizers to thrive. After harvesting, cut off tops for first-rate compost, and leave roots in the soil to release their nitrogen.

RUNNER BEANS One of the most decorative and tastiest vegetables.

How to grow: In mid-spring, sow singly, 2in (5cm) deep, in cell trays. Plant out in early summer, either against canes in double rows 12in (30cm) apart, or against a wigwam with 12in (30cm) between canes. Alternatively, sow direct in late spring, two seeds per cane; leave strongest seedling. Water freely in dry weather.

Harvesting: Pick regularly to ensure steady supply.

Best Bets: Antique 'Painted Lady', with ornamental red and white flowers; stringless 'Kentucky Blue'; 'Scarlet Emperor'.

FRENCH BEANS, DWARF Dwarf bush beans are prolific and can be grown singly in containers.

How to grow: Sow successively direct into moist, warm ground from late spring to mid-summer, at three-weekly intervals. Sow seeds 2in (5cm) deep, 6in (15cm) apart, 9in (23cm) between rows.

Harvesting: Pick regularly when young and tender, from 4in (10cm) long.

Best Bets: 'Masai', slim filet beans; early 'Aramis', slender flat pods; 'Purple Teepee', purple pods, green when cooked; waxy, yellow 'Gold Crop'.

FRENCH BEANS, CLIMBING Same as dwarf beans, but taller, and need staking. The choice is yours.

How to grow: As for runner beans.

Harvesting: While beans are young and tender, from 6in (15cm) long.

Best Bets: 'Blue Lake White Seeded', 5ft (1.5m) stems; 'Borlotto Lingua di Fuoco', flamboyant red-streaked pods.

SUGAR SNAP PEAS I prefer sugar snaps to podding peas; with these, you eat peas plus their plump, sweet pods. They have a better flavor than flatter-podded snow peas. Grow short varieties for ease of care, and to save on space.

How to grow: Sow quite thickly when soil is warm, in late spring to early summer, in shallow drills 4in (10cm) wide, allowing 12in (30cm) between rows. When plants reach 4in (10cm) high, support with plastic netting and pea sticks. Protect from birds with black mesh stretched along rows.

Harvesting: Pick sugar snaps when pods are plump, and approx 3in (7cm) long; they fade fast if left on stem.

Best Bets: 'Honey Pod'; 'Oregon Sugar Pod III'; 'Sugar Gem'.

SWEETCORN Each plant produces only one or two cobs, and you'll need space to grow even half a dozen, but that freshly picked taste is well worth it.

How to grow: Choose a sunny sheltered site for growing. Sow under glass in mid-spring, three seeds to a 3in (7cm) pot. Thin to strongest seedling. In early summer, plant out 24in (60cm) apart each way, in blocks, not rows, so that plants pollinate.

Harvesting: When tassels at the top turn brown; use immediately.

Best Bets: 'Sweetie'; early F1 'Champ'.

POTATOES If I could only grow one vegetable, it would be the potato; the taste of a freshly dug steamed baby potato is better than caviar.

How to grow: For a small space, you need only a few tubers (seed potatoes); each tuber will produce at least 1lb (450g) of potatoes. They must be 'chitted' which means leaving them, 'eyes' up, in an egg box in a cool, light place until the eyes have sprouted, after four to six weeks. Plant in spring, sprouts upwards, 4in (10cm) deep and 12in (30cm) apart; if in rows, 24in (60cm) apart; cloche or cover to protect against cold. Keep well watered. As foliage grows, 'earth up' stems to avoid poisonous green potatoes. Foliar feed after eight weeks.

Harvesting: When foliage has died down, after two to three months, grub around in the soil for your potato crop. Keep a few back and replant, growing as before, in ground or container. Protect

Decorative and delicious runner beans such as antique variety 'Scarlet Emperor' add cottage garden charm to the vegetable plot, especially when planted to clamber up a rustic wigwam.

against frost from autumn onwards and harvest before ground freezes.

Best Bets: Early varieties such as waxy 'Early Gem' and 'Superior'; peanut shaped 'Giant Peanut Fingerlings'. Later, disease-resistant 'Russet Sebago', buttery 'Yellow Finn', high yield 'Red Sun'.

BEET GREENS Related to beetroot and easier than spinach which runs to seed in hot weather. Usefully gives greens for winter, and spring. Also known as perpetual spinach and chard.

How to grow: In spring, for summer cropping, sow in drills 1in (2.5cm) deep, each drill 12in (30cm) apart. Thin seedlings to 6in (15cm) apart. Sow in mid-summer for fall cropping, cloching to keep leaves tender.

Harvesting: Start picking leaves when 3-4in (7-10cm) long. Use as for spinach.

SPROUTING BROCCOLI For decorative value, grow this tasty vegetable in the flower border; each plant grows up to 36in (90cm). For warmer parts of the country.

How to grow: In spring, sow thinly, ½in (12mm) deep, in a seed bed outdoors, and thin to 3in (7cm) apart. When plants are 3in (7cm) high, transplant to final positions, 20-24in (50-60cm) apart, watering planting hole beforehand. Plant deeply and stake.

95

Harvesting: From late winter to spring, when broccoli heads start sprouting. Cut central head first, to encourage sideshoots. *Best Bets:* 'Purple Sprouting Early' and 'Late White Sprouting White Star'.

SWISS CHARD Dark green Swiss chard is delicious, but ruby chard is gorgeous; 24in (60cm) high, stems a glowing shade of beetroot.

How to grow: In mid-spring, sow 1in (2.5cm) deep, 12in (30cm) apart each way, placing two seeds in each hole and thinning to strongest seedling; sow in mid-summer for autumn cropping. Water freely in dry weather.

Harvesting: Pull outer leaves from base to encourage fresh growth. Midribs, steamed, can be eaten separately.

Best Bets: 'Rhubarb Chard'; 'Lucullus'.

TOMATOES Patio tomatoes, sweet and aromatic take up little space; larger types must be supported.

How to grow: In mid-spring, sow in warmth, two seeds ½in (12mm) deep to a 3in (7cm) pot; thin to strongest seedling. When plant is at least 3in (7cm) high, transplant to sunny position or 10in (25cm) pot (dwarf varieties, 6in (15cm) minimum). Spacing for patio plants, 18in (45cm); full size plants, 30in (75cm). Provide central cane for support. For vining varieties, pinch out sideshoots in leaf axils when they appear, and tie stem to cane as it grows. When you see fruit on the fourth truss up stop, i.e. pinch out the growing tip, two leaves higher. Water well and regularly. Erratic or over-watering can cause fruits to split, rot or worse. Feed weekly with tomato fertilizer or liquid seaweed or fish emulsion, and remove yellow leaves. *Harvesting:* Pick as tastebuds dictate.

Best Bets: 'Gardener's Delight', F1 'Sweet 100', orange F1 'Sungold' (all cherry tomatoes); stripy tomato 'Tigerella';

Many garden designers incorporate ruby chard into their planting schemes amongst flowering perennials. The rich red stems and veined leaves are an ornamental asset, and when you tire of them, you can eat them.

'Big Beef'. Compact bush varieties, F1 'Pixie', 'Tiny Tim', F1 'Totem', early, oval-fruited 'Super Roma UF'; and trailing F1 'Tumbler', ideal for hanging baskets.

SALADINGS

Keep salads crisp and tasty with these easy-to-grow essentials.

LETTUCES Big-headed butterheads, thick-leaved crispheads, cut-and-come again decorative loose-leaf lettuces offer a mélange of color and texture for the salad bowl. Spice up blander varieties with peppery arugula leaves or herbs.

How to grow: Sow little and often, from early spring to early autumn, ½in (12mm) deep, in narrow drills. Keep soil moist through growing period. Thin seedlings gradually to eventual final spacings of 6in (15cm) for small

lettuces, up to 12in (30cm) for crispheads. For containers, sow in small pots and transplant when small. In very hot weather, which lettuces hate, sow several to a cell in cell tray, and keep in shade. Thin to strongest seedling per cell, plant in shady bed and keep moist.

Harvesting: From ten weeks. Loose-leaf lettuces should be snipped when leaves are young; leave a little to sprout again, or pick entire leaf. Head lettuces should be picked with stalk attached if not to be used right away.

Best Bets: 'Beatrice', reliable frilly crisphead; small-scale butterhead 'Tom Thumb'; compact cos 'Little Gem'. Loose-leafed, frilly 'Lollo Rosso' (red), 'Lollo Bionda' (green), green and red 'Salad Bowl'. Loose-leaf mixes, 'Mesclun', 'Saladin' and 'Misticanza'. Make autumn sowings and cloche for spring supplies of 'Little Gem', 'Lobjoit's Green Cos', 'Valdor'.

RADISH Goodbye to store-bought pliable, flavorless radishes, hello to home-grown, juicy-crisp and peppery.

How to grow: Successively from early spring through summer, covering first sowings. Sow ½in (12mm) deep, spacing seedlings 1-2in (2.5-5cm) apart.

Harvesting: Only four to six weeks after sowing. Pull and twist off tops if not eating right away.

Best Bets: Quick-growing, oval 'French Breakfast'; round 'Cherry Belle'.

SPRING ONIONS Sow from spring to the start of summer, successively, to ensure good supply of this piquant salad ingredient to the end of summer.

How to grow: Sow thinly, ½in (12mm) deep in blocks or rows, ½in (12mm) apart and leaving 3in (7cm) between rows.

Harvesting: Pull when pencil-thick, but can be left to grow larger and harvested when needed.

Best Bets: 'White Lisbon'; red-skinned 'Santa Claus'.

ARUGULA Peppery rocket is delicious on its own or tempered with milder salad greens. Pick when young, or taste gets too hot to handle.

How to grow: In seed trays, containers, open ground, from spring to early autumn; in summer heat, sow in shade. Sow thinly in shallow drills, cloching early sowings.

Harvesting: Start snipping when plants are 3-4in (7-10cm) high, leaving some leaf behind, and they'll regrow.

EXOTICS

Sow something different, including your own supply of tangy watercress.

EGGPLANT One of the most decorative – and delicious – vegetables. Grow in a container, in the sunniest spot on the patio.

How to grow: In mid-spring, sow three seeds to a 3in (7cm) pot, and thin to strongest seedling. After about six weeks, transplant into a 8-12in (20-30cm) container, depending on size of variety, and secure to cane. Pinch out growing point when plant is 10-12in (25-30cm) high. Water regularly, and liquid fertilize when fruits have started to swell. When five fruits have set, or about fifteen of smaller varieties, remove sideshoots and rest of flowers.

Harvesting: Cut off each fruit while it is plump and still shiny.

Best Bets: 'Bambino', fruits just 1in (2.5cm) long; 'Elondo Hybrid', elongated fruits; F1 'Easter Egg', ivory-colored fruits.

CHILLIS AND SWEET PEPPERS Chillis and sweet bell peppers are ideal container plants, but need heat to ripen.

How to grow: In mid-spring, sow three seeds to a 3in (7cm) pot, and thin to strongest seedling. After about ten weeks, when first flower truss has started to form, transplant into a 8in (20cm) container, and secure to a cane. Pinch out growing point at the top of plant. Keep watering, and liquid feed when fruits start to swell.

Harvesting: Cut fruits from stem when fully grown and green, or allow them to color yellow or red. Sweet peppers will keep for weeks; chilli peppers eventually shrivel.

Best Bets: Sweet bell peppers, F1 'Jingle Bells'; F1 'Redskin'; dark 'Purple Beauty'. Chilli peppers, 'Anaheim', mild; F1 'Super Cayenne', long, slim, yellow, red hot; 'Tabasco Habernevo', slow-burn sweet pepper that heats up as it matures.

FLORENCE FENNEL The aniseed taste of these crisp bulbs is distinctive and delicious.

How to grow: Sow direct in drills, ½in (12mm) deep, 12in (30cm) apart, in mid-spring. Thin to 9in (23cm) apart. Earth up the bases as they swell to the size of golf balls, and continue to earth up until they reach tennis-ball size, at the end of the summer.

Harvesting: Cut base with sharp knife.

Best Bets: 'Herald'; 'Fino'; 'Romy'.

WATERCRESS No need for running water to grow watercress: buy a fresh bunch and root in a jelly glass, then space small plants 4in (10cm) apart in large pot of soil. Keep the pot standing in water. Change water daily, twice daily, in hot weather.

STOPPING TOMATOES

If you are growing long vine tomatoes, remember to keep pinching out the sideshoots that appear in the leaf axils, so that the plant's energy is directed into the fruit-bearing stems.

ORIENTAL VEGETABLES

Look in the seed catalogues for increasing numbers of Chinese and Japanese vegetables. Aside from their culinary cachet, they have few pests and diseases, are rich in vitamins and minerals, and taste equally good raw, steamed or stir-fried. Many can be sown in summer to pick soon after and right through the late autumn. Some to try: white mooli radish, Chinese chives, succulent pak choi, chop suey greens (garland chrysanthemum), mizuna greens, 'Beauty Heart' radish, which has green skin on the outside, pink and white flesh on the inside.

97

PLANNING YOUR VEGETABLE PLOT

WRITE IT DOWN

Protecting crops, sowing successionally, using varieties which mature at different times, catch cropping and transplanting, will all help make your vegetable plot work hard and long throughout the season. Decide on what you want to grow first, read what follows, and then plan out the plot on paper. Don't worry if you can't keep every corner constantly busy, that's asking for too much. Better to grow a few varieties well than a dozen indifferently. Keep this year's plan for reference next year; you think you'll remember where everything was, but you won't.

CROP ROTATION

Grow the same vegetable in the same space every year, and you deplete the soil of the same nutrients, and build up pests and diseases. The three-year crop rotation plan is simple and worth following. Even if you grow vegetables in odd corners, follow the principle: don't grow crops from the same family, on the same site, for two successive years.

The three basic groups are: Peas and Beans, Brassicas, Roots. Fruiting vegetable plants are less fussy, but grow them in different spots every year. Group 1 (Peas and Beans) includes spinach and spinach beet, sweetcorn, zucchinis, lettuce and all salad plants. These benefit from rich, manured soil. Group 2 (The Brassicas) include broccoli, cabbage, calabrese, cauliflower, kohlrabi, radish, turnip. Group 3 (The Roots) include beet, carrot, celery, garlic, parsnip, potato, salsify. Group 1 fixes nitrogen into the soil, so upping the fertility level. Follow Group 1 crops with Group 2 which benefits most from absorbing that nitrogen. Brassicas loosen

98

CROP ROTATION OVER THREE YEARS

Bed Ⓐ   Bed Ⓑ   Bed Ⓒ

Bed Ⓐ   Bed Ⓑ   Bed Ⓒ

Bed Ⓐ   Bed Ⓑ   Bed Ⓒ

up the soil, which neatly brings in Group 3; root vegetables love to dive down into that loose soil, and should not be grown in ground that has been recently manured

CATCH CROPPING

This is the knack of growing two crops successively on the same patch of ground in one year. You can use quick-growing catch crops in the summer space vacated by slower growers started earlier, such as lettuce after purple sprouting broccoli. You can also start out with quick crops early on, then clear them for late crops such as spring cabbage and other winter brassicas, which you sow in late summer.

INTERCROPPING

When slower-growing crops such as brassicas are small, grow quick-growing crops in between the rows, to harvest before the slow growers have matured. Small lettuces, radishes, baby beet, baby turnips, finger carrots and arugula are just six that could fill the spaces. Don't overdo intercropping, or the quick crops will become troublesome weeds to the others. When climbers such as runner beans have barely begun their ascent up a wigwam, quick crops can be grown in the center. Zucchinis and French beans can be grown around sweet corn, which takes up vertical space only, and gives little shade.

SUCCESSIONAL SOWINGS

Many quick-growing vegetable varieties can be sown several times in one season, so that as one crop is harvested, another is maturing. Extend the period, too, by starting earlier under polytunnels or clear plastic tarp, and warming the ground beforehand with same. When weather cools, protect once more, cloches on tomatoes, summer squash, peppers and eggplants will also hasten ripening.

QUICKER CROPPING

Small vegetable plots can be worked intensively by stepping up growing cycles. How? Grow vegetables closer, thin less than usual; close neighbors also keep vegetables stylishly small. Choose suitably compact varieties where possible; harvest when young, tender and tastiest, between 8-12 weeks.

99

HERBS

The dilemma you face with chives is whether to keep snipping them for salads, or let them flower to use as a valued decorative edging plant for the border. The solution is probably to grow enough chives to allow you to do both. The flowerheads are tasty too.

You might not like the taste of thyme and you might prefer your pizza without oregano. No matter, because although herbs are indispensable in cooking, as well as cosmetics, medicine and aromatherapy, many of them make ravishing aromatic – make that aromantic – ornamentals for the garden.

HOW TO GROW HERBS SUCCESSFULLY

Most herbs need similar conditions, which makes it easy to site a herb garden, and get the soil in suitable shape. Consider their native habitats, and you'll understand their needs: warm, sunny sites with very well-drained soil – so work in plenty of grit or sharp sand before planting if soil is heavy. If you can't provide these essentials, grow herbs in large containers in any sunny corner: instant Mediterranean!

Watchpoint: Unlike most plants, herbs thrive without feeding. In fact, poor soil brings out their finest flavors and aromas.

WHICH HERBS TO GROW?

The herbs below are ones I consider must-haves – but in time you'll discover more that you couldn't possibly be without.

BASIL (*Ocimum basilicum*) Grow basil from seed; supermarkets may sell the stuff in cheesy little pots, but who can have enough basil in summer? True, it can be temperamental but sow in warmth, water during the day to avoid damping off, only bring the young plants outdoors when the temperature rises in early summer, and it should thrive. Sow successionally through summer for fresh plants; grow in a guaranteed hot and sunny spot and don't let it wilt to death. Basil buffs argue the merits of small-leaved Greek (*O. b. minimum*) versus large-leaved Italian (*O. b. neapolitanum*): both are great. Purple basil (*O. b. purpurascens*) has style, and purple ruffle-leaved basil (*O. b.* 'Purple Ruffles') will leave your dinner guests speechless with admiration.

BAY (*Laurus nobilis*) This handsome evergreen tree can be grown as a pyramid, standard or simply free-form. It also looks terrific in a large terracotta pot – a good growing option as it is not winter-hardy in the north. To keep in shape, clip in late spring and late summer, when you will have an abundance of bay leaves for the cooking pot.

CHIVES (*Allium schoenoprasum*) For snipping over salads, the young, green shoots of chives are indispensable, but some would argue that the chunky pink flowering heads, edging a border, are equally indispensable; the choice is yours. Good herb choice for a windowbox. Chives grow from tiny bulbs; dig up clumps and divide every two years or so.

CORIANDER (*Coriandrum sativum*) Essential for exotic cooking, coriander is best grown from seed because the young, fresh foliage is what is needed;

besides, it's easy to raise from seed sown in spring. Grow it in a patch, or pots, but keep cutting, or it will bolt and be useless. *Watchpoint:* buy the variety best for leaves, not seed: some catalogues helpfully call it *C. s.* 'Cilantro'.

MINT (*Mentha*) Let mint loose and it will run rampant, so keep it under control by containing the roots in pots sunk in the ground. Keep different varieties separate, because one is likely to overpower the other, physically and aromatically. Mint will grow in sun or shade. Finest for tea, and cooking, is verdant Moroccan mint (*M. spicata* 'Moroccan'); most decorative is less rampant pineapple mint, *M. suaveolens* `Variegata' with cream-edged, hairy leaves that smell of pineapple.

OREGANO (*Origanum*) You say oregano, I say marjoram, and to add to the confusion, there are so many varieties that even the experts don't agree on their names. But whichever you choose, all the oreganos make spreading flowering mounds, about 12-18in (30-45cm) high, that are an asset to bed and border edges as well as containers. Good for flavor are Greek oregano (*O. vulgare spp*), with gray-green leaves; golden marjoram (*O. vulgare* 'Aureum') with lime-gold leaves (also a useful foliage plant and good alongside purple sage). Trim after flowering to keep plants bushy, and cut back before winter to within 2-3in (5-7cm). Mound layer as for thymes if plants get bare at center.

PARSLEY (*Petroselinum*). Grow parsley from seed in spring and summer if you want substantial supplies. For smaller quantities it's easier and inexpensive to buy a potful or three. Parsley likes rich soil and lots of water, so grow in light shade, whether in ground or container, and keep snipping.

ROSEMARY (*Rosmarinus*) This is no teeny windowsill herb. Grow rosemary bushy and billowing as a fine-looking evergreen; especially good beside a path where you can brush past and appreciate that fragrance, as well as clip generous sprigs for the cookpot. *R. officinalis* is the commonly grown rosemary, with pale blue flowers in spring; *R. o.* 'Miss Jessopp's Upright' is just as it sounds, and there are also rich blue, pink and white-flowered rosemaries. Use prostrate rosemaries to tumble and trail over the edges of walls,

It's a pity to hide herbs away in the vegetable plot, when so many of them make aromatic and highly ornamental additions to the border. Top left, reading clockwise: sage, fennel, santolina, thyme and marjoram.

hanging baskets and containers. Sun and well-drained soil are vital for rosemaries; use as outdoor shrub in Southern areas, grow in pots in the North. Trim after flowering.

SAGE (*Salvia*) Purple-leaved *S. officinalis* 'Purpurascens', gold-splashed *S. o.* 'Icterina' or cream, pink and green *S. o.* 'Tricolor'. Sorry to be mundane, but my favorite is the common sage, *Salvia officinalis* itself, because of that lovely, er, sage color, because of the chunky purple flowers in summer, and because it's the best sage for cooking. Prune in spring to encourage fresh young growth, and trim after flowering. Mound layer as for thymes if plant gets woody at center, and replace straggly plants after a few years.

THYME (*Thymus*) These herbs are mat-forming (prostrate varieties), clump-forming (upright, bushy varieties), and they're habit-forming, too. How to choose between gray woolly *T. pseudolanuginosus*, mauve-flowered, pungent *T. vulgaris*, variegated *T. v.* 'Silver Posie', lemon-scented *T. citriodorus*? You don't have to, because deliciously aromatic thymes are small enough for you to grow them all: on sunny banks, at path edges (and in paving cracks) or as a tapestry carpet. Plant with lots of grit, cut them back after flowering, and rejuvenate weedy plants that have grown bare in the middle by, in spring, mounding soil, sharp sand and shredded bark at center; new shoots will grow through.

101

FRUIT TREES

Now that compact fruit trees are so widely available, even the smallest of gardens can boast its own ornamental – and productive – orchard. It's more fun, though, to grow fruit all over the garden: as fans against house walls, trained over arches, or even as little step-over trees by path or border. You'll have fruit, foliage and ravishing spring flowers.

KNOW YOUR ROOTSTOCK

Your first consideration when buying a fruit tree? Not the variety, but its eventual size. Today, fruit trees start life as two separate units, grafted together: the scion and the rootstock. (This explains the 'family' apple tree, where several different varieties are grafted onto one rootstock!) The scion is a shoot from the fruit variety, and the rootstock is the root system that dictates the ultimate size and vigor of the tree. Both these factors should influence your choice. If you don't want a spreading apple tree, you must have a dwarfing rootstock. Rootstock M27 produces the smallest apple trees at 4-6ft (1.2-1.8m), M9 trees of 8ft (2.5m), and MM106 trees a height of 12-16ft (3.6-4.8m). Pixy is the rootstock for small plums and peaches; Quince C for pears up to 10ft (3m). Colt and Inmil roostocks will produce compact cherry trees that fruit within two years of planting.

Note: dwarfing rootstocks demand rich, fertile soil.

WELL-TRAINED TREES

Next consideration is the shape or form of the tree. Yesterday's gardener would have to train a one-year-old tree himself. Now ready-formed trees, fully trained at a few years old, can be bought from the nursery (for best choice) or garden center, and most are on dwarfing rootstocks. Highly ornamental, space-saving, quick to produce fruit and easier to maintain, they add great style to the humblest plot.

Note: Cordons, espaliers, step-overs and fans must be supported by horizontal wires for support, either free-standing between posts, or against a wall or fence.

BUSH With short trunk and open center, the bush variety is quick to fruit and easy to maintain. Don't plant in grass.

STANDARD Half standards have a longer stem, at least 4ft (1.3m), and standards at least 6ft (1.8m); these are tall trees on vigorous rootstocks that are suited as lawn specimens.

ESPALIER This form has several horizontal tiers of branches on either side, spaced about 1ft (30cm) apart. One tree looks good, and a row of them in a kitchen garden (plant 10-12ft (3-3.6m) apart) looks stunning. Apples and pears only.

STEP-OVER At about 15in (37cm), tops, they're almost trip-overs, and perfect for path and border edgings, planted 5ft (1.5m) apart. Step-overs are like espaliers, except they have just one branch on either side of the stem. For apples, pears and plums.

FAN Branches radiate outwards in fan shape. Plant 10-12ft (3-3.6m) apart. Ideal for peaches, plums, cherries and pitted fruits because they crop best when grown against a sunny wall.

PYRAMID For free-standing apple, pear and plum trees, the pyramid shape tapers towards the top, so that picking and maintenance is easy. Plant about 5-6ft (1.5-1.8m) apart.

CORDON This useful form is a single, straight stem with fruiting spurs along its length, grown at an angle to restrict sap flow and thus encourage fruiting. Cordons are perfect for the small garden, because they can be planted only 30in (75cm) apart; one won't yield a huge amount of fruit but plant a mixed row and you're in business. For apples, pears, and berries.

FESTOONS Classic method in which the young branches of apples, pears or plum trees are bent into a hoop shape, so that the branches produce many shoots along their length. These shoots are then pruned back to form fruiting spurs.

COLUMNAR TREES Ideal for containers and small spaces, these 6-8ft (1.8-2.5m) trees have barely-there sideshoots and need no pruning. If you would like a maypole of blossom or fruit, they are for you. Originally apples only, columnar pears, plums and cherries now available. Plant 30in (75cm) apart.

GROWING POINTS

❀ Buy as containerized plants, to plant at any time, or bare-rooted (sometimes rootballed, when roots are burlapped) for planting in the dormant period.

❀ Make sure your chosen tree is free of pest or disease, and check that the graft union, which will appear as a slight bulge, is smooth and well-healed.

❀ Plant all fruit trees, especially against walls or fences, with plenty of retaining organic matter such as well-rotted compost or manure, as well as a generous handful of general fertilizer, and mulch. The graft union should be above soil level.

❀ Free-standing trees should have a strong stake knocked into the planting hole (*see Chapter 3, p. 48 for details*).

❀ Mulch and fertilize in early spring. Water generously with a hose when fruit is swelling

❀ Net trees if you'd rather the birds didn't eat the entire crop. Use traps to catch codling moths, and sticky bands to deter winter moths (*see chapter 9 for fruit tree pests and diseases*).

❀ All tree fruit detailed below will crop in containers, but must be watered and fed copiously from spring to autumn.

PRUNING

As a guideline for all fruit trees, aim for an evenly spaced framework that forms an open goblet shape. Every year shorten main branches by about one third, and to encourage fruit, shorten all branches' sideshoots to about three buds.

Prune cordons in summer by cutting back woody-based mature shoots growing from the main stem to 3in (7cm), and any new growth from sideshoots to 1in (2.5cm), just above the leaf cluster at the base. When the cordon has reached required height, cut back annually as you would a sideshoot.

Prune espaliers in summer by shortening sideshoots to about 3in (7cm), and any shoots from these to 1in (2.5cm). Treat step-overs the same.

Prune fan-trained apple and pear trees in summer by removing new

A well-trained fruit tree not only looks magnificent, but will produce the optimum amount of fruit to follow the blossom. This gorgeous fan-trained morello cherry has the virtue of flowering and fruiting even on a cool north wall.

CLIPPINGS

✄ Blossoms damaged by frost will affect fruit yields later in the year. Prevent this by choosing later-ripening varieties, and protect the flowers with plastic sheeting when frost is forecast.

✄ In the first year, nip out the flower buds of young apple trees to prevent fruit forming, so trees direct energy to getting established.

shoots growing towards or away from supports, and prune each branch as for cordons. (For fan-trained plums and cherries, see below.)

APPLES Least fussy of all tree fruits, apples will grow in most reasonable conditions, though they will perform best in a sunny, sheltered site with rich soil. Aside from the good old orchard tree, grow apples as cordons, espaliers, festoons, fans and step-overs. Grow two varieties in the same, or near, flowering period for pollination; a crabapple will pollinate most apple trees in flower at the same time ('Brandywine' has a very long flowering period), and a neighbor's tree might do the job.

Pruning: In late winter, remove crowded and crossing branches and useless twigs, aiming for an open goblet shape. Cut back branches by one third. Instead of pruning young trees, encourage fruiting by pulling down branch tips and tying them to the trunk, or directing vertical branches more to the horizontal.

Best Bets: There are so many varieties available that it is best to look and try for yourself, at harvest time. Your criteria are flavor, cropping, good disease resistance. Consider modern, disease-resistant varieties such as 'Mac Free', 'Freedom' (cannot pollinate another variety) and 'Jonafree' a good new cooking apple. 'Enterprise', 'Gold Rush' and 'Royal Gala' are three tasty

disease-resistant varieties that will pollinate each other and provide fruit from late summer to winter.

CHERRIES Sweet cherries crop best when fan-trained against a warm house wall. Trees must be netted to protect against birds. Plant them in a sunny, sheltered site that is not in a frost pocket.

Pruning: Prune fan-trained sweet cherries as for plums.

Best Bets: Most need a partner to pollinate, although sweet cherries 'North Star' and 'Stella' are self-fertile.

FIGS A sunny site is essential; a fan-trained fig against a warm wall will always give the best results. The roots must be restricted if you want your fig to fruit, so when planting make a large hole and fill the bottom and sides with rubble, allowing only the smallest cracks for water to drain through. Must be wrapped in cold winter areas. Not hardy North of New York City (Zone 6). Don't allow your fig to dry out, especially while it is establishing.

Pruning: In summer, pinch out sideshoots beyond four leaves to encourage fruit production. Thin out overcrowded young shoots and remove any baby figs before winter to conserve tree's strength. (Don't worry, new figs will form in spring.)

Best Bets: For wall, 'Brown Turkey'; as a bush, 'Italian Honey'.

PEARS Susceptible to late frosts, pears are best grown as fans, espaliers or cordons against a sunny wall or fence where they have a sheltered position. They also prefer slightly acid soils that are rich and moist. Some varieties are partly self-fertile, though they will give better results if pollinated. Choose two or three from the same, or near, pollination period.

Pruning: As for apples.

Best Bets: Early autumn, 'Bartlett',

'Moonglow'; mid-autumn, 'Seckel'; early winter, 'Beurré D'Anjou'. New, compact 'Colette' is early, with excellent flavor; 'Beurré Bosc', 'Red Barlett' and ever-popular 'Clapp's Favorite' are all garden-worthy choices that will pollinate one another.

PLUMS Grow plums, greengages and damsons as bushes, half standards, or as fans against a wall. All these fruits need rich soil with masses of organic matter, and won't tolerate poor, dry conditions. Be patient: you may have to wait several years before your plum trees bear fruit. If the crop is heavy, thin fruit after the pits have formed; you might even, lucky thing, have to support the branches.

Pruning: Plums fruit on both old and new wood. For bushes or trees, cut out dead and spindly branches in early spring or after harvesting. For fans, in spring, first remove any shoots growing toward or away from supports. Then select the sideshoots you want to fruit, which should be about 3in (7cm) apart, and tie them in. Pinch out their tips after they have made six or seven leaves. After harvesting, shorten shoots by half.

Best Bets: You might need two to tango, depending on your choice. All damsons are self-fertile. Popular 'Stanley' is self-fertile, and so are the following: compact cooking plum, 'Fellemberg'; yellow-skinned 'Yellow Egg'; flavorful greengage 'Imperial Gage'.

FRUIT FOR COLD REGIONS

Most fruit need frost-free springs for good crops and full flavour. But in a cold climate the following will all crop well: red lake currants, north star cherries, empires and northern spy apples, blueberries, Russian mulberries.

BERRIES AND CURRANTS

Strawberries are easy to grow provided they have fertile, well-drained soil in a sunny position. If necessary, protect the crop from slugs and snails. They grow well in containers, providing a limited but worthwhile crop.

Fruit cages make ideal safe harbors for berries and currants, but there are more decorative ways of growing these delectable hardy fruits. Grow strawberries in your windowbox or Japanese wineberries over the arbor. New varieties may be more compact and easier to manage, but they haven't, thankfully, lost out on flavor.

GROWING TIPS

❊ All berries are self-fertile, so will crop without a partner.

❊ Best time to plant fruit canes and bushes, which are usually sold bare-rooted, is in autumn, when soil is still warm.

❊ All varieties benefit from well-prepared soil laced with lots of organic matter, plus a general fertilizer and a mulch when planting.

❊ Mulch and fertilize every spring, and give regular high-potash liquid fertilizer during the growing season. Foliar feeds are beneficial too. Keep plants well watered when fruit is swelling.

❊ The berry's biggest enemy: birds. Grow fruit under netting; humming wires, even scarecrows, can be effective. (*See Chapter 9 for pests and diseases, and how to get the better of them.*)

❊ Make sure you buy your berry bushes from a reputable source and buy certified virus-free stock where possible, as poor stock is likely to carry disease.

❊ Most berries do well when grown in tubs, except raspberries, blackberries and their hybrids.

PROPAGATING METHODS

Blackberries and their hybrids can be tip-layered; take hardwood cuttings of gooseberries and currant bushes. Raspberries produce suckers; these can be dug up and replanted. Strawberrries produce baby plants at end of runners; alpine strawberries can be grown easily from seed.

BLACKBERRIES Fruit best in sunny, sheltered site with rich, moist soil. Plant canes in early autumn, spacing plants 8-10ft (2.5-3m) apart. After planting, cut back to a bud about 9in (23cm) from base. Train against horizontal wires 12in (30cm) apart, attached to posts in open ground, or to vine supports on a fence. To keep the new shoots away from the old, fruit-bearing canes, tie in fruiting canes on one side, and new growth on the other.

Pruning: Cut out fruited canes at ground level, and position and tie in strongest current-year canes. *Best Bets:* Blackberry, 'Choctaw', terrific flavor; 'Thornfree', thornless late cropper. 'Chester' and 'Navaho Erect' are

RASPBERRY CANES

As raspberry canes grow, they will need to be supported. Do this either by stretching horizontal wires between posts or to support attached to a wall or fence and tie in the canes with soft string.

Buy blueberry bushes as container-grown rather than bare-rooted plants. For best results, mulch well to help keep the soil moist. An ideal choice for containers, blueberries need to be grown in ericaceous compost to thrive.

compact, fruitful and thornless; the stout canes can be grown wigwam style in the border. Hardy to Canada is 'Illini', a medium-size, very flavorful fruit. Ready to harvest in August.

ELDERBERRY North American shrub 6-10ft (21.8-3m). Easily grown anywhere to Northern Canada. Prefers damp soil but not fussy, as can be seen growing wild along road sides and damp embankments. No serious pests or diseases. Flat ivory flower clusters attractive to butterflies in midsummer, then black-purple berries in late summer, attractive to birds and good for jam and elderberry wine. Propagate from suckers, which plant produces quite freely.

Pruning: Only if it overgrows location.

Best Bets: Species still most common, but hybridizers have begun to show interest. There are golden-leafed varieties.

BLUEBERRIES One bush will crop, but for best results, plant two different varieties that will cross pollinate. Can eventually reach 6ft (1.8m). A good container choice, especially as blueberries require lime-free soil; grow in ericaceous (acid lover's) soil with plenty of compost. If your soil is suitably acid, plant bushes 5ft (1.5m) apart. Water with rainwater preferably.

Pruning: Not needed in first few years, but you can control the bush by cutting out old wood in winter.

Best Bets: Early-fruiting 'Patriot'; 'Ivanhoe', large fruits; 'Bluecrop'.

CRANBERRIES Like blueberries, cranberries demand acid soil; they also need permanent moisture, so are only worth growing if you can site them by waterside or in boggy conditions on peaty soil.

KIWI FRUITS Vines 10-30ft (3-9m) with heart-shaped leaves. Prefers full sun and good garden soil. Best trained against a wall, fence or over an arbor. Lime green flesh; flavor compared to a blend of strawberry and pineapple. Fruits store several months in refrigerator. No significant pests or diseases. Male plant needed to pollinate New Zealand varieties.

Pruning: Remove dead vines in spring.

Best Bets: Hardy Japanese Kiwi 'Issai', compact, smooth skin, very sweet flavor, will survive to -20°F (-29°C); 'Hayward', fuzzy New Zealand type ripens late October.

RASPBERRIES Summer varieties fruit on one-year-old canes; autumn varieties, on current-year shoots. Raspberries prefer a sunny, sheltered site with slightly acid, fertile and well-drained soil. Mulching and regular watering is important. Plant canes 18in (45cm) apart, and shorten right away to a bud 9-12in (23-30cm) above soil level. As canes grow, support with horizontal wires stretched between posts or against a wall, the canes tied in with twine.

Pruning: In the first spring after planting, cut out any weak canes to near ground level. After fruiting, cut out old canes of summer varieties to near ground level; tie in the strongest of the new canes at 4in (10cm) intervals, cutting out weaker canes. Cut canes of autumn-fruiting forms to ground level in late winter.

Best Bets: Early fruiting, 'Titan', thornless, some disease resistance; mid-summer, 'Mammoth', thornless, good disease resistance; late summer, 'Killarney', extra hardy to Canada, some disease resistance, excellent flavor; autumn, 'Lowden', yellow 'Fallgold', both heavy croppers.

STRAWBERRIES Choose from four categories: large, summer-fruiting (considered the best flavored); everbearing, which fruit in summer and autumn; tiny-fruited alpines, fruiting from early summer to late autumn, and new 'day neutrals' (not dependent on daylight to fruit) from the US, which crop from summer to first frosts. Grow in a sunny, sheltered site with fertile, well-drained soil. Plant summer and autumn fruiting varieties in summer; day neutrals and alpines in late spring. Space 12-15in (30-37cm) apart, keeping crowns at soil level. Remove annual weeds by hand. Feed in spring with high-potash fertilizer and keep well-watered. Allowing runners to make more plants will increase yield, but fruits will be smaller, so either leave runners to root, or cut them off. Berries resting on the soil are problem-prone, so grow through strawberry mats or tuck straw under plants as fruit ripens, to protect against slugs. After summer-fruiters have cropped, shear off old leaves; remove old leaves of perpetuals and day neutrals. Burn or discard the straw, but don't put it on your compost heap. For maximum cropping, replace

Raspberries are arguably the finest of all the summer berries. Autumn varieties are especially easy to grow and provide valuable late fruit. Always buy from certified virus-free stock and keep plants well watered and mulched in the growing season.

summer-fruiting varieties after three to four years; autumn-fruiting varieties and day neutrals, every other year. Use a fresh planting site when putting in new plants to avoid picking up disease.

Best Bets: Early, 'Honeoye', 'Annapolis'; mid-summer, 'Redchief', 'Guardian'; late mid-summer, 'Scott', 'Seneca'; everbearing, 'Tristar', 'Ozark Beauty'; day neutrals, 'Tribute'; alpine, 'Shades of Pink', novel 'Pineapple Crush'.

UNUSUAL BERRIES

Hybrid berries such as boysenberry, dewberry, dingleberry and youngberry are all flavorful offspring of blackberries and raspberries. Grow them as you would blackberries, although hybrids prefer full sun. Japanese wineberries are especially decorative. The gooseberry has a tart, green or purple fruit that is used for pies, jams and condiments. 'Pixwell' is the most common variety.

107

THE WILDER SIDE

The good news is that you can introduce a few wildflowers without having to dig up the rose bushes. Impatiens and jewel weeds can co-exist in harmony. By simulating, even on a small scale, marsh, woodland or open field, you welcome their inhabitants, and give the garden another dimension. The bonus: your garden will have a better ecological balance. So lay down your weed wacker (you might harm a bunny). Forget tightly clipped hedges (no knowing who lives there). Cultivate a few untidy corners. Let roses have their hips, lawn have its daisies. You might consider a wildflower meadow hard work (it is). But you could turn a patch of turf over to thyme for a fragrant carpet, or plant flowers for their scent. You'll bring in butterflies and bees — like bees to a honeypot. Carve out a pond for frogs, toads, birds and insects; even a bowl sunk into the ground or upturned trash can lid will serve as a watering hole. Lastly, learn the secret of successful wildflower gardening: recreate a habitat that simulates the plants' natural home. And learn to love weeds. Well, some of them.

MAKE YOUR GARDEN BUZZ...

bergamot

borage

fried egg plant

pot marigold

tortoiseshells especially), wild marjoram (keep cutting back to provide flowers and continuous nectar supply), perennial asters (*Aster* x *frickartii*), golden rod (*Solidago*).

SPECIFIC FOOD FOR BEES

Bee balm or bergamot (*Monarda*), foxglove, globe thistle (*Echinops ritro*), clover, meadow crane's bill, asters, penstemon, feverfew (*Centaurea scabiosa)*, broom, heather.

GROW A BUTTERFLY BREEDING SITE

To welcome butterflies into your garden a friendly gesture would be to cultivate a special weed patch for their benefit. Certain trees will also bring them in. Caterpillars of moths and butterflies such as the monarch depend on the common milkweed for survival, while blues love clover, viceroys like poplars and willows, and black swallowtails love parsley or celery.

Common milkweed *(Asclepia incarnata)* thrives in damp spots and the large-podded seeds are easy to collect and grow. Its orange-flowered relative is aptly called butterfly weed (*Asclepia tuberosa)* and, in contrast, prefers a dry sandy location, but both plants will do very well in any good garden soil.

SOME FLOWERS THAT ATTRACT BENEFICIAL INSECTS

Fried egg plant, pot marigold, scabious, Californian poppy, fennel (the wide flat flowerheads are a draw), *Sedum* 'Autumn Joy', hyssop, aster.

...with bees, butterflies and other beneficials. Provide nectar-rich flowers such as honeysuckle, sedum, buddleia and evening primrose in your garden, and they'll bring in the butterflies and bees, the finest of fruit pollinators. Just as important, they'll attract hoverflies, which look like small wasps, but are harmless, and ladybugs. Not only are both these insects pollinators, but their larvae will feast off your aphid population. Beats using sprays any day.

SOME PLANTS THAT ATTRACT BEES AND BUTTERFLIES

Many wildflowers, and flowering herbs, provide rich food sources for both bees and butterflies. These include borage, bugle (*Ajuga*), primrose, cornflower, milkweed, forget-me-not, thrift, Joe Pye weed, flowering thyme, evening primrose, yellow flag, ox-eye daisy.

Both bees and butterflies also love lavender, hyssop, sea holly (*Eryngium*), fried egg plant (*Limnanthes douglasii*), scented honeysuckle.

SPECIFIC FOOD FOR BUTTERFLIES

Provide a balance through the year, focusing on summer and autumn, when there are most butterflies.

SPRING Golden alyssum, aubrieta, sweet rocket.

EARLY SUMMER Catnip, honesty, valerian.

MIDSUMMER Mallow, pot marigold, candytuft, musk mallow, broom, Queen Anne's lace.

LATE SUMMER Buddleia (prune later in spring, and it will flower later, when more butterflies are around; keep on deadheading to encourage more blooms), *Sedum spectabile* (another major hit with butterflies, small

BEST WILDFLOWER PLANTS

Woodland plants favor cool, shady sites, while meadow and grassland flowers prefer open ground and sun. (*For annuals see p. 115.*)

BIENNIALS

Plant biennials in autumn. Alternatively, sow seed in late summer directly into the ground or else into pots to plant out in the spring.

FOXGLOVE (*Digitalis*) Prefers a position in part-sun, part-shade. Pink, white, purple flower spires in early summer. Can reach 4ft (1.2m).

VIPER'S BUGLOSS (*Echium vulgare*) Purple and blue flowerheads, expansive foliage. Sun. Long tap root so withstands drought; 24in (60cm)

SWEET ROCKET (*Hesperis matronalis*) Flowers early summer. Airy drifts of white or violet flowers that grow fragrant toward evening. Self-seeds. Sun or semi-shade; 3ft (90cm).

HONESTY (*Lunaria annua*) Flowers in spring. Mauve or white flowers but honesty is valued most for its decorative opalescent seedheads, beloved by birds too. Up to 3ft (90cm).

FORGET-ME-NOT (*Myosotis sylvatica*) Clumps of pale blue flowers mid-spring; self-seeds everywhere, but easy to pull. Low-growing.

EVENING PRIMROSE (*Oenothera biennis*) Flowers from early summer. Full sun. Fragrant yellow flowers open at dusk, last one day; 3ft (90cm).

PERENNIALS

Sow seed of perennials in autumn and plant out in spring. Alternatively, buy as plugs or plants.

CHAMOMILE (*Anthemis arvensis*) Very fragrant daisy-like flowers with fine, feathery foliage. Can be used to make chamomile tea. Sun; 12in (30cm).

LOBELIA (*Lobelia siphilitica*) Native prairie plant that flowers medium to light blue. 30in (80cm).

JOE PYE WEED (*Eupatorium purpureum*) Prefers moist, sunny meadows. Dusty pink clusters from July onward. To 12ft (3.6m).

RED VALERIAN (*Centranthus ruber*) Lovely flowering plant that will grow profusely in border as well as in the tiniest path cranny. Red, pink and white varieties; 30in (80cm).

CRANE'S BILL (*Geranium sanguineum*) Good foliage and plentiful flowers of a wonderful cool cerise. Self-seeds. Up to 12in (30cm).

BEE BALM (*Monarda didyma*) Mauve, red or white shaggy crowns on 2-3ft (60-90cm) stalks. Good wildflower for growing in meadows.

Foxgloves produce their charming and familiar flower spires from early summer in shades of pink, purple and sometimes white. They are natural woodlanders and self-seed with ease.

OX-EYE DAISY (*Chrysanthemum leucanthemum*) Tall white daisy that inhabits wildflower meadows. Grows from seed. Sun, semi-shade; 24in (60cms).

PERENNIAL FLAX (*Linum perenne*) Pale blue flowers, dainty foliage on thin stems. Needs sun. Looks good on path edges and self-seeds with ease; 12-24in (30-60cm).

BEARD TONGUE (*Penstemon*) 'Prairie Fire' bears scarlet tubular flowers on airy plants. Sun or semi-shade. 30in (80cm).

MUSK MALLOW (*Malva moschata*) Bushy plant with dainty foliage, pretty pink flowers. Musky scent. Sun or semi-shade; 24in (60cm).

OBEDIENT PLANT (*Physostegia virginiana*) Pink or white flowers in late summer and fall. Makes runners in damp soil. Sun or semi-shade; 3ft (90cm).

JOHNNY JUMP-UP (*Viola tricolor*) Pretty wild pansy with yellow and violet flowers. Short-lived perennial, so best treated as an annual. Good in gravel paths and in the front of mixed borders; 8in (20cm).

BULBS

Many of the smaller-flowered species tulips work well with wildflowers. The star of Bethlehem is widely sold but it can be rather invasive. *Scilla siberica* provides a daintier option for small gardens. Dwarf daffodils suit woodland beds and the old-fashioned poet's daffodil (*Narcissus poeticus*) and the *triandrus* narcissi, such as 'Hawera' are ideal for naturalizing in long grass.

Always buy wildflower bulbs from a reputable bulb merchant; they should be cultivated, not dug up from the wild.

111

BRINGING IN THE BIRDS

Birds can be pests to plants, granted, but their diet includes aphids, caterpillars, snails and destructive insects. And anyway, birds are such lively, tuneful garden visitors that who wouldn't encourage them?

Actually I wouldn't, and can't, because of my two predatory cats, but you might be luckier. If I could, I'd have a roofed bird feeder, but just for the cold months; in spring and summer, birds forage for slugs and aphids, and besides, babies might choke on kitchen scraps and nuts. I'd site it near dense shrubs so shy birds would use it, too, and load it with a running buffet selected from seed mixes, cheese, nuts and fats, bacon rind, moist bread and cake. Water for drinking and bathing is important, too.

If you don't have your fair share of inviting tree hollows, you could put up a nest box for birds (I daren't). Site it high in a tree, on a climber-covered wall or fence, or anywhere high up, safe from disturbances (including you: one peek, and the birds could desert their new-found nest).

Windfall fruits such as apples, pears and plums may make the garden look untidy when left to lie on the ground, but they are greatly appreciated by birds, wasps and butterflies at different times of year.

A good variety of trees and large shrubs in the garden provides shelter, shade, roosting and nesting sites, as well as song perches. Thick climbers against walls encourage birds to nest. Dogwood and willow stems are potential habitats, too. Some birds have even been known to set up home in large, flower-filled hanging baskets. Ivy provides winter shelter, as well as crannies to house insects that wrens feed on and autumn nectar for butterflies. Berried shrubs such as holly, cotoneaster, berberis, *Viburnum opulus* and pyracantha, and trees such as rowan and crab apple, provide autumn and winter food, as well as spring nesting sites.

Bird-friendly gardens have their fair share of rose hips, nuts and seedheads left on herbaceous perennials by thoughtful owners. Ripe teasel seeds are adored by goldfinches; autumn-flowering asters and rudbeckias should be allowed to keep their heads, and sunflowers make the ultimate feast: cut the dried heads off and hang them from trees in the dead of winter when they're most needed. And if you want to watch true pecking order among your garden's bird population, plant mullein and Scotch thistle for their seed heads as well as their flowers.

LEAFY HABITATS AND COSY CORNERS

Even a small garden can be an adventure playground for small animals, as well as hold inviting hideaways for them to snuggle up in and maybe hibernate, uninterrupted. Leave some stones invitingly laid over hollows for toads and newts, slow worms even, as well as centipedes, which, hallelujah, prey on slugs. Pile up a few logs – they need only be small – in a shady, out-of-the-way spot, and very soon beetles, spiders, bees, slugs and snails will be proud to call this damp log cabin home; you could plant it with native ivies and ferns. And with those inviting creepy crawlies on the menu, blackbirds and wood mice will call it a restaurant. At night, you might get skunks coming to forage for insects and slugs. Incidentally, skunks slurp up slugs, which is a good enough reason to make them feel cosy with a box of straw or an inviting pile of leaves, and to leave them a dish of pet food, out at night. Do not surprise them when you are doing so.

HOW TO MAKE A WOODLAND BED

Your woodland bed might not become a preferred opossum and skunk hangout, but it could well become your favorite corner of the garden. After all, it's a bare-faced excuse to house some of the most bewitching springtime bulbs and plants.

Choose a site that has some shade lent by deciduous trees and background shrubs (wild roses, viburnum and holly provide berries and hips for woodland visitors), and is not facing the sun. You can create ideal dappled shade with atmospheric, small-scale trees. Perfect for creating the enchanted woodland atmosphere, and lending a sense of scale, are the squiggly-branched hazel tree, *Corylus avellana* 'Contorta', that in spring is decked with dangling lemon catkins (supplying pollen at a welcome time of year), and baby pussy willow, *Salix caprea* 'Kilmarnock', with cascading branches to create fine woodland theatre.

Before you plant, you need to get the soil in suitable spirit. Think of the woodland floor, rich and moist from a continuous mulch of leaves. Create a near-enough equivalent by forking in masses of shredded bark to provide the necessary well-drained, moisture-retentive soil.

Start planting with the largest woodlanders, the hellebores. Plummiest – in both senses of the word – is *Helleborus orientalis*, which boasts saucer-shaped blooms from dusky plum to palest green, sometimes plum-speckled, hanging from plum-flecked stems; snip back the spear-shaped leaves to better display the flowers. The Christmas rose (*H. niger*), has pristine white blooms, sometimes spattered with red; dramatic *H. foetidus* alias the

stinking hellebore – for reasons which will become clear to you – has masses of small cup-shaped ice-green flowers each rimmed with damson. Give hellebores space, and watch for seedlings; replant them where you would like them to settle. Divide hellebores in spring, when clumps get overcrowded.

Pulmonarias, or lungwort, are compulsory in the woodland bed, and, like hellebores, they flower early and go on for ages. Their foliage forms impressive clumps, frequently marbled with silver or white, and the small flowers start out pink and change to blue. Tug off the outer leaves if they threaten to conceal the carpet of *Cyclamen coum*. These dainty originals of the flashy hot pink houseplants, with tiny wavy flowers ranging from white to magenta, put in their appearance each spring by pushing up curly, plum-colored stems and marbled leaves.

In light shade, tuck in a few *Anemone nemorosa*, the daisy-shaped pink and white windflowers. You could fill your woodland bed with the mellow yellows and fresh greens of the common primrose, *Primula vulgaris*, with colorful *Polyanthus* and drumstick primroses for added variety. There will barely be room for violets: *Viola odorata*, the sweet violet, exquisite dog violet, *V. riviniana,* and somehow, you must also leave space for foxgloves.

In early autumn, get bulb planting: choose yellow and lilac crocuses to

Salix caprea 'Kilmarnock'

Helleborus foetidus

Helleborus niger

Pulmonaria 'Sissinghurst White'

Anemone nemorosa

naturalize under the trees, and plant drifts of dainty dwarf daffodils all over the place. Bluebells would be good, too; look for the mouthful *Hyacinthus amethystinus* in the bulb catalogues, or daintier *Scilla siberica*. For some really special effects, plant a few bulbs of the gorgeous woodland Martagon lily (*Lilium martagon*), which has dangling turkscap maroon flowers. Or look for the native *Lilium canadensis* with tawny caps.

For the final touch: a do-good mulch of leaf mold, coarse-chipped bark or even cocoa shells, with an enticing way through the woods, if need be, made of cut-log stepping stones.

113

LAWN TODAY, MEADOW TOMORROW

Just a small patch of your clipped lawn converted to a swishing-in-the-wind wildflower meadow could be a haven for wildlife and a stunning natural feature. Even buttercups and daisies, given their own way, have great charm.

primroses and violets. Let the grass grow a little, not too much, or you won't see the flowers.

You could, of course, sow a wildflower meadow from scratch – small scale, you understand – by using a prepared mix of wildflowers and grasses. If you love hard work, you could lift the lawn, prepare the soil underneath and take it from there. It might be tempting to go for wildflowers alone in your thirst for color, but they look more natural mixed with grasses, which also provide food for caterpillars, a habitat for small creatures and place for butterflies to lay their eggs.

You could plump up the meadow mix in the same way as converting a lawn to meadow status, by plug planting. Any wildflower prefixed with 'corn', 'field' or 'meadow' is suitable. Perennials will give you a longer display than the brief but beautiful cornfield annuals, so plant as many as you can, in autumn. Musk mallow, Joe Pyeweed and coneflower are three essentials. Plant annuals at the same time (or sow in pots the previous autumn, plant in spring), and encourage them to self-seed by leaving the cuttings after mowing, as well as raking the ground; wheatfield annuals thrive on disturbed ground, which is why they spring up after the grain is cut. Plant plenty of spring- and summer-flowering bulbs such as wild daffodils, snakeshead fritillaries, if the soil is not dry, and dainty *Allium ostrowskianum* which have spear-like leaves and rich cerise flowers. (Incidentally, Prince Charles has two tones of hybrid tulips in his wildflower meadow and they look terrific; if he can do it, so can you.) Cut a swathe – well a path – through your meadow with

A wildflower meadow is hard work. Leaving the grass to grow under your feet will not do, unless you're a fool for couch grass and enraptured by dandelions. Nor will flinging wildflower seeds around help, because the grass will simply crowd some wildings out, while others won't even germinate.

The way that works is to plant young plants of wildflowers in weed-free turf, with a bulb planter. And if you haven't religiously fed your lawn, so much the better, because wildflowers

thrive on poor soil, which is why so many self-seed in paving cracks and gravel paths. You'll have a better chance of cornfield annuals self-seeding if your lawn is patchy and poor – they're unable to compete with dense turf. Raking beforehand to pull out thatch and disturb ground will help.

Awkward-to-mow corners of the lawn make ideal miniature meadows, but only if they are in the sun and not shaded by trees. In these areas, you could add woodlanders such as

A WILDFLOWER BORDER

Somewhat easier than simulating a wildflower meadow is making a wildflower border; poppies and cornflowers will establish more readily on bare earth. In autumn or spring, simply sow a wildflower mix direct, sow patches of different wildflowers, or compose natural drifts with precision plug planting. If your wildflower border is next to your lawn, and you hold back on mowing, you will find some border immigrants setting up home among the grass.

frequent lawnmower runs; the lawnmower's width is all you need. The ongoing battle, though, will be keeping the bad weeds down, and the good weeds going; unless you're a botanical genius you'll need to wait and see before pulling out most seedlings. Stand by annually with replacement plug plants, fresh seed of annuals or collect your own seed, (*see Chapter 5, p. 85*).

MEADOW MAINTENANCE

Time for complete cutting down is late summer, when the wheatfield annuals have finished flowering. Use a rotary mower set at the highest cut, so that the finished height is 3-4in (7-10cm). Leave the cuttings lying for a day or three for the seed to fall (and the wildlife to settle; we're talking insects, not buffalo), then rake them up and toss on the compost heap. You'll need to make a few more cuts before winter if you don't want a savannah out there.

If your meadow peaks in spring, with fritillaries, primroses and the like,

cut it back when they have finished flowering and their leaves have turned brown, and keep the grass at a manageable length through summer.

MEADOW ANNUALS

Annuals can be sown in spring, but for a head start sow them early in the previous autumn, in poor soil (they don't like it rich). For best control, sow in pots and plant out in spring on raked ground. Planting them between perennials, in sunny borders, is ideal. Make sure to plant in drifts, not dots, or the effect will be parking lot plantings, not grassy knoll.

PHEASANT'S EYE (*Adonis annua*) Southern meadow beauty with dark-centered scarlet flowers and decorative leaves. But won't establish in grass. About 12in (30cm).

CORN COCKLE (*Agrostemma githago*) Grow pretty pink-flowered corn cockle amongst other meadow annuals, not just because it

complements, but because it needs support. Sunny site. Can reach a height of 4ft (1.2m).

CORNFLOWER (*Centaurea cyanus*) Popular garden wildflower, with intense blue flowerheads (sometimes white, pink and purple). Self-seeds on bare soil. Grow with flowers such as poppies for support. Up to 36in (90cm).

CORN MARIGOLD (*Chrysanthemum segetum*) Long summer flowering period. Self-seeds readily. Golden daisy-like flowerheads, bushy foliage. Up to 20in (50cm).

LARKSPUR (*Consolida ambigua*) Feathery leaves and spikes of intense purple-blue flowers. Glorious with mixed wildflowers. Up to 24in (60cm).

FIELD POPPY (*Papaver rhoeas*) Lovely scarlet petals make the Memorial Day poppy essential for the wildflower patch. Self-seeds in cultivated soil, but won't naturalize in grass unless the ground is disturbed annually. Up to 24in (60cm).

For a bolder alternative to daisies dotting the lawn, sow perennial *Chrysanthemum leucanthemum*, the ox-eye daisy that frequents open meadows, into bare earth as part of a cheery wildflower border. Ideal companions are blue cornflowers and scarlet poppies.

CREATIVE PLANTING

In the following pages you will find ideas to help you plant your garden with flair and spur you on to greater creativity. A word of advice before you begin. Decide on your garden's overall personality, and don't allow yourself to get sidetracked. Great gardens were not born from the ragbag look, a combination of styles born out of indecision. Work within the limitations of what you have and go for the looks you love, not something you feel other people might approve of. Look at pictures of gardens or better yet, the real thing and see which stir your soul. Are you a fool for formal gardens with box hedging, manicured lawns and lots of statuary? Contemporary gardens, with modernist sculpture and expressive, architectural plants? English country gardens, with sumptuous borders heavy on the herbaceous? Wild gardens, with native hedging, berry-bearing bushes and thorny roses? Within such broad categories lies masses of scope for introducing your own personal touches and spirited plantings, painting your own bright canvas, and having enormous fun as you go.

PLANTING POINTERS

An unpromising shady corner of the garden offers many planting possibilities provided you do not expect a riot of colour. Focus on foliage of diverse textures and cool shades of green. Hostas for example, provide handsome leaves that look as if they are finely quilted.

❀ Chances are you're taking on somebody else's garden. They might have been a devoted plantsperson (lucky you) or they might have had a thing for unbroken lawns (start digging). Ideally wait and see what buried treasures come up over the seasons before making major overhauls.

❀ Place plants in the best positions for them to thrive, and they're likely to work together without jarring (you're sure to hit on some stunning effects, and those you like less, you can always change later).

❀ Sometimes conditions in one area of the garden will dictate the style of planting there. If part of your garden is boggy, consider a small-scale, lush, leafy jungle with hostas, ferns and moisture-loving flag iris.

❀ A sunny bed with stony soil cries out for Mediterranean planting. Search out plants of that region, such as aromatic lavenders, rosemaries, hyssops and helichrysums, along with sun-loving bulbs of species tulips, alliums and madonna lilies. Mulch with grit. Simple and stunning.

❀ To make a border really sing, you need to site a plant not only where it feels comfortable, but where it looks terrific and makes its neighbors look good, too. Don't drive yourself crazy over this. Aim for simple, eye-pleasing groupings, each one with plants that have a similar flowering period, so you vary the moment of glory with each grouping, rather than each plant.

❀ Consider the eventual shape and height of shrubs and perennials when planting, so that you can give them adequate space, and choose complementary neighbors. Will the plant spread out like wildfire? Will it grow in a space-saving slender column? Will it be a compact dome, an abject sprawler, or an all-out weeper?

❀ The predictable border has tall plants at the back, which makes sound viewing sense, but shake things up by planting the occasional tall, airy plant bang in front, such as bronze fennel, *Verbena bonariense* or tall alliums.

❀ Balance a border with diverse shapes and textures. Two neighboring plants with similar foliage shapes will tend to blend and lose impact. Mix up hummocky mounds (*Armeria maritima, Dianthus*) with verticals (lupins, hollyhocks), with airy-fairy plants (foam-flowered *Thalictrum,* baby's breath *Gypsophila*), with lush, large leaves (hostas, bergenia), and with spikes and spears (iris, crocosmia). In small beds, lots of verticals will have the effect of making the space seem larger.

❀ Avoid the itty-bitty amateur look by planting, where feasible, in threes and fives (odd numbers look more natural than evens). Even in a small space, two or three big plants carry more impact than lots of small plants.

❀ Plant almost anything *en masse* and it looks wonderful: a mass of sunflowers, a shady walkway bordered with towering white campanulas.... An iron will is vital here. You might find salvias irresistible, but a purple sea of common *Salvia* x *superba* is more striking than a drift of seventeen different ones; go for the big picture, not for a national collection.

❀ Once your framework is planted, don't attempt to fill the border right away; you're not a garden designer on a rush job. If you hate the look of bare earth, top it with bark chippings.

❀ You won't get it all right first time. Some things will obscure others; some might not grow fast enough; some might keel over and die. Most plants can be moved, so take out what doesn't work, and move it somewhere better. Eventually the three bulbs will form a drift, the hellebore will outgrow its space. The fascination for all gardeners is that the picture is constantly changing.

❀ Allow the garden to throw its own design curves. Often the best compositions are unplanned and come about by chance; for instance, vagrant orange marigolds amongst purple osteospermums; white *Malva moschata alba* popping up along a colorful border and giving it unity; succulent-like *Euphorbia myrsinites* wiggling out from a crack in the walk.

❀ Be cheered by the fact that very few colors in the garden look truly awful together (although you never saw the red-and-white striped 'Ferdinand Pichard' rose I planted next to the purply-brown berberis), and note that the closer you keep to nature, the more likely it is that the colors will harmonize. When did you ever see clashing colors in the countryside?

❀ If you do get stuck with two plants that clash, take the cheat's way out: plant forgiving foliage between the two.

SPECIALS TO SOW

❀ Honesty and aquilegia usefully fill the gap between spring and summer. Sow them in autumn and you'll always have them. After flowering, pull most of them out (leave a few to seed) to make space for summer flowers.

❀ Once sown, blue nigella and the opium poppy *Papaver somniferum,* which both have showy, sculptural seedheads, will seed with abandon.

❀ Two papery poppies make great gap fillers: yellow Welsh poppy *Meconopsis cambrica,* orange and pink Californian poppy *Eschscholzia.*

CLIPPINGS
✂ Visit gardens, private and public (take a notebook and camera); even the grandest borders will have copiable cameo plantings that may appeal to you.
✂ If you're starting from scratch, drawing a rough plan to indicate the plants, their flowering times, colors and shapes is helpful.

A forest of fennel, which self-seeds with abandon, adds an atmospheric veil to the border. Use it in front of an interesting plant to throw the foreground out of focus and shift the emphasis on the plant behind.

119

COLOR HARMONY

If you're cautious about color, the classic color spectrum will throw you a clue or two about which colors work well together. Harmonizing partners hug one another in the color wheel: thus you can see that red and purple are good together, as are purple and blue, and blue and green, which softens down to lemon and continues to yellow, through to orange, then scarlet and back through purple. You can also use the color wheel to check out good contrasting partners by seeing which are opposite each other: blue and orange, purple and yellow, red and green. Colors approaching orange are warm; colors nearer to blue are cool. Keep plant groupings to all-warm or all-cool, and they won't jar. Those hot, jazzy

colors (reds, oranges, golds) stimulate and energize; cool, pastel colors (blues, grays, pinks, greens, lemons) are easy on the eye and have a restful quality. So far, so cool, but truth is that plants offer trillions more color nuances than paint, and are far more exciting to work with. Looking at the color wheel won't inspire you to place gunmetal with purple-black, but seeing moody maroon tulip 'Queen of the Night' next to the outsize, gray, sharply-cut leaves of the cardoon in a late spring border, will.

USE COLOR CREATIVELY

Many gardeners use the brightest plants in their borders but balk at painting so much as a garden seat. Bringing in color

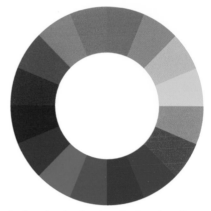

Look at the classic color wheel, and you'll discover which colours make interesting partners, such as purple and yellow. You will also be able to see which colors harmonize with one another, such as purple and red, and blue and green.

by painting garden features (furniture, trellis, arches, etc.) a strong, sure shade displays plants to the max and ensures a cheering vista year-round. Paint woodwork of the house exterior, the garden gate if you have one, the same color, too and you connect the house with garden, seamlessly. A leafy green garden takes off when underscored with touches of crisp white on bench, gate or archway, but soft sea-green is the best color going to complement plants. Use it to paint garden railings, outside paintwork, a garden seat (whether wood or metal), a cluster of terracotta pots. Or, in the Southwest, do as designer Yves St Laurent has done in his Moroccan garden, use several shades of singing, strong blue, including deep royal and turquoise, to give your garden immense style and energy. Stain the garden fence leaf-green and you're halfway to covering it with evergreen climbers. Color-wash a cheerless brick wall with palest apricot, and grow lipstick pink roses up it. Paint the trellis backing the violet-flowered clematis a buff lemon. And if, in the end, you tire of sky blue pink, simply paint it over the following season.

Plants are not the only way to introduce vibrant colour to the garden. Paint backdrops, furniture, accessories in complementary colours, and don't be afraid to change them seasonally. They'll provide a stylish foil for your plants and add interest in the lean months.

MONOCHROMATIC BORDERS

Neither monotone nor monotonous, the monochromatic border incorporates many colors to give the impression of one, and proves that a dozen degrees of one color group look more effective in a small space than a dozen different ones. Contrasting textures, shapes and heights all play important roles in the monochromatic border. It's great fun to work on, and could be used, of course, just in a small plant grouping.

THE BORDER BLUES

No wonder we're all mad for blue flowers. Not only is it hard to find enough variety to confine yourself to a true blue border (you'll slide helplessly into lavenders and mauves), it's a shame to confine these perfect partners away from so many other plants. Don't deprive yourself. In springtime, imagine sky-blue grape hyacinth *Muscari armeniacum*, and piercing blue dwarf Iris reticulata among the lime-green leaves of *Alchemilla mollis* and vibrant golden grass *Milium effusum* 'Aureum'. Picture (better yet, plant) gentian-blue *Delphinium belladonna* 'Wendy' alongside the flat yellow heads of *Achillea* 'Moonshine'; deep blue hyssop flowers at the base of rich striped pink *Rosa gallica* 'Versicolor' ('Rosa mundi'). And for a gorgeous late summer-flowering bulb duo, match deep blue agapanthus to orange crocosmia. Sow blue borage and orange pot marigolds to come up together, alongside a patch of *Veronica austriaca teucrium*

'Crater Lake Blue' in high summer. The richest blue perennial aside from delphinium is *Anchusa azurea* 'Loddon Royalist', a tall flower spike of luscious sapphire-blue. And the big blue backdrop to contrast with golds and yellows: ceanothus.

THE SIZZLING RED-HOT BORDER

Almost creates itself in late summer, when flower colors of intense reds, golds and coppers predominate, preparing us for the richer autumn tints that are to follow. Picture (if you dare) red-hot pokers *Kniphofia uvaria* in flame and yellow, copper-red *Helenium* 'Moerheim Beauty', vermilion *Dahlia* 'Bishop of Landaff', towering scarlet *Lobelia cardinalis*; fire-engine-red *Crocosmia* 'Lucifer', and statuesque *Canna* 'Roi Humbert', which has lipstick-red flowers and deep purple foliage.

Bank up the fire (as if it needs it) with supporting bronze foliage of *Heuchera micrantha diversifolia* 'Palace Purple', *Ajuga reptans* 'Braunherz', spiky *Cordyline australis* 'Purpurea', bronze phormium, and claret-coloured vine *Vitis vinifera* 'Purpurea'. An all-red border will focus on foliage earlier in the year, so you might prefer to use just a group of these firecrackers to spice up the border in late summer.

THE FOREVER SUNNY YELLOW BORDER

Incorporates lemon, butter-yellow, sulphur-yellow, gold, apricot, lightened with lashings of cream. To a backdrop of green and yellow evergreens (including golden variegated holly, *Choisya ternata*, *Euonymous fortunei* 'Emerald 'n' Gold', and *Euphorbia characias*), the yellow players stroll out steadily through the year, kicking off with winter-flowering jasmine. In spring, there are cream and yellow primroses, crocuses and daffodils;

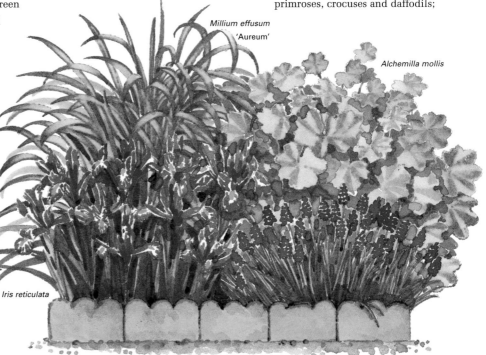

Millium effusum 'Aureum'

Alchemilla mollis

Iris reticulata

Muscari armeniacum

121

Match plant colors together as you would pieces of fabric. Instead of playing safe, try and include adventurous color combinations, such as this stunning and off-beat duo of red valerian and cinnamon iris 'Kent Pride' with golden furry throat.

chrome-yellow alyssum *Aurinia saxatilis*, and bedding wallflowers; 'Golden Apeldoorn' tulips. *Cytisus* x *praecox* 'Allgold', and creamy *C.* x *kewensis* provide late spring pzazz; potentillas butter-yellow 'Moonlight' and coppery 'Tangerine' continue to flower right throughout the whole summer; while yellow-flowered honeysuckle *Lonicera* 'Graham Thomas' lights up the shade.

Add English rose 'Graham Thomas', planted among high summer perennial flowers, lemon *Achillea* 'Taygetea', rich yellow *Verbascum chaixii*, and soft yellow foxglove *Digitalis ambigua*. Include day lily *Hemerocallis* 'Stella de Oro', endlessly flowering yellow daisy *Anthemis tinctoria* 'E. C. Buxton', golden evening primrose *Oenothera fruticosa* and *Osteospermum* 'Buttermilk'. Before the sunny yellows settle down, coreopsis, *Rudbeckia fulgida* 'Goldsturm', and goldenrod (*Solidago)* shine on.

THE SUMPTUOUS COLOR PURPLE

Deep, dark and sultry, the purple border incorporates mauves, violets and crimsons, but the mood can be lightened at will with uplifting silver and pink. Begin with a few broody backdrop shrubs such as purple smoke bush *Cotinus coggygria* 'Royal Purple', gray-mauve stemmed *Rosa glauca*, *Berberis thunbergii atropurpurea*, deep violet *Buddleia davidii* 'Black Knight', lifted with lavender-blue *Clematis* 'General Sikorski', and double *C.* 'Royalty'. Start the year innocently enough with baby pink and magenta *Cyclamen coum* and lilac crocuses, violet *Viola cornuta* 'Velour Purple', and muted mauve double primroses. In late spring, *Camassia esculenta*, and arching purple broom *Chamaecytisus purpureus* flower, while the tall, fuzzy spheres of mauve *Allium aflatunense* mixed with dark wine *Tulipa* 'Queen of the Night' tower above magenta cranesbill *Geranium*

sanguineum. The purple passion reaches its peak in high summer with a profusion of smoky-purple sage, gray-stemmed, cerise-flowered *Lychnis coronaria*, dusky crimson *Rosa rugosa* 'Rubra', *Penstemon* 'Sour Grapes', blackcurrant-colored cone heads of *Allium sphaerocephalon*, metallic-mauve sea holly *Eryngium bourgatii*, moonlit-lilac *Salvia sclarea turkestanica*, and the deepest purple-robed heads of *Aconitum avendsii*. Sensational.

THE EXQUISITE WHITE BORDER

Is only exquisite if tinted liberally with silver, gray and blue; otherwise it is the flat and dreary white border. Complementary foliage plants such as *Festuca ovina glauca*, 'Elijah's Blue', felty-gray *Stachys byzantina*, *Ruta graveolens* and *Hosta* 'Blue Moon' are essential. *Lamium maculatum* 'White Nancy' makes good variegated white ground-cover for shady spots, along with white *Geranium* x *cantabrigiense* 'Kashmir White'. For spring, kick off with creamy white narcissi, *Pulmonaria officinalis* 'Sissinghurst White', *Viola cornuta* 'Alba', white honesty *Lunaria annua alba*, lily-flowered white *Tulipa* 'Triumphator'.

In summer, *Clematis* 'Marie Boisselot' provides huge paper-white flowers, and 'Iceberg' roses are ravishing. Philadelphus is essential in the all-white garden, as is sweet rocket *Hesperis matronalis*, frothy gypsophila, regale lilies and tall, white, scented tobacco plant *Nicotiana sylvestris*. Sprinkle liberally with self-seeding *Malva moschata alba*, annual *Lavatera* 'Mont Blanc', and blue and white love-in-a-mist. Silvery-lilac echinops and eryngium, irridescent blue delphiniums, white-stemmed perovskia, and soft blue bellflower *Campanula persicifolia* all

Gray and silver foliage, such as felty-leaved *Stachys byzantina*, gray-leaved sage and silvery thyme, link colour groupings together in the border, and look equally effective teamed with white flowers like this kniphofia and glaucous-leaved sedum.

heighten the ethereal quality. There are zillions more choices, and it has been said that the white border hardly presents a challenge, but why would you worry? It sure is pretty.

COLOR CONNECTORS

Use foliage in drifts or ribbons through the border to link color groupings together. Green is the most undervalued garden shade, yet if two plants don't connect, a patch of foliage between them provides the missing link. Gray and silver foliage plants are invaluable when it comes to linking diverse pastel shades. Try gray *Stachys byzantina* 'Silver Carpet', aptly called lamb's ears, meandering through a border; lace-like *Artemisia* 'Powis Castle' and steely, shimmering *Verbascum olympicum* between shrubs and perennials (and as knockout plants in their own right). Herbaceous *Artemisia ludoviciana*, which appears to have been carved from pale gray felt, looks terrific flirting in and around leggy roses.

On a smaller scale, plant small, silky hummocks of blue-gray grass *Festuca ovina glauca* 'Elijah's Blue' between plants (site it next to black ribbon grass *Ophiopogon planiscapus* 'Nigrescens' for real impact!) Purple sage is perfect for connecting pinks and blues (plant *Lathyrus latifolius* alongside, and let those delicious pink flowers ramble through). Apple-green *Alchemilla mollis*, frothing through a border, links just about everything together, so do streams of easy-going *Geranium* x *endressii* 'Wargrave Pink' in and around herbaceous perennials. You can also use drifts of go-with-everything soft blue flowers as color connectors: forget-me-nots in spring (they self-seed to reappear the following year), hazy clouds of catmint, or love-in-a-mist in summer.

123

DOUBLE ACTION PLANTING

Sow summer annuals among herbaceous plants to fill in the gaps, and to provide good color contrasts. To set off hazy mauve catmint, vibrant orange Californian poppies and soft blue love-in-the-mist are left to self-seed and flourish.

❀ Plant hybrid lilies close to early flowering shrubs, to flower later among their foliage.

❀ Use perennial sweet peas to romp over ground where earlier plants have finished flowering; they will charmingly cover all kinds of mess.

❀ Plant soft mauve *Allium aflatunense* to soar through golden shrubs such as *Philadelphus coronarius* 'Aureus', and later-flowering deep maroon *Allium sphaerocephalon* to do likewise through silver shrubs such as santolina.

❀ Plant *Dicentra spectabilis* among hellebores, so the flowers on their long, dangling stems in late spring will take over the flagging show.

❀ Unfurling leaves of hostas among spring bulbs will cover their faded foliage in late spring.

❀ In California and Arizona gardens, plant hardy fuchsias such as *F.* 'Checker-board' with white and magenta flowers, *F. magellanica*, with new foliage marbled with cream, pink and green, and *F.* 'Autumnale', with single scarlet and purple flowers, green and yellow foliage that takes on coppery autumn tints, to take over from spent bulbs and early fizzers. Cut hard back in spring. Best compact fuchsia for front of border: 'Tom Thumb', which drips with red and purple dangling flowers in summer.

❀ Oriental poppies leave a gap in high summer which can be taken over by later-flowering stars such as Japanese anemones and mauve daisy *Aster* x *frikartii* 'Mönch', planted near by.

❀ Conceal a few fireworks under the workaday ground-cover geranium. For instance, underplant 'Johnson's Blue' with bulbs of early double tulip 'Peach Blossom', and golden day lily *Hemerocallis* 'Stella de Oro'.

When one plant has finished performing, another takes over, distracting the eye... clever stuff when you know how.

❀ The easy way of ensuring action more than once a year in the border: bulbs! Under deciduous trees or shrubs, and yet-to-emerge herbaceous plants such as peonies and crane's bill geraniums, you could have primroses and *Anemone blanda* (which helpfully disappears after flowering), dwarf daffodils, blue grape hyacinths, tulips. In turn, those herbaceous plants will cover the bulbs' fading foliage.

❀ Plant crocuses, grape hyacinths and species tulips to come up through ground-cover plants such as ajuga, lamium, *Stachys byzantina* and thymes, and among the wiggly stems of low-growing succulent *Euphorbia myrsinites*.

GOOD PLANT PARTNERS

You don't need extra special plants to create extra special effects.

🌸 These three garden center regulars make terrific bedfellows: *Euphorbia characias wulfenii* (gray-blue evergreen with flowerheads of sulphur-yellow whorls in spring), *Dianthus plumaris* (gray-leaved perennial with very fragrant pink flowers from spring on), and *Potentilla fruticosa* 'Katherine Dykes' (yellow flowers for months in summer). Underplant them with equally available, cheerful grape hyacinth and dwarf daffodils.

🌸 Informal grouping for light shade: *Rosa glauca* with gray-mauve stems, small pink flowers and dark hips at the back, fronted by pink *Hydrangea* 'Preziosa' and *Berberis thunbergii* 'Rose Glow'. In between, pink Japanese anemone *Anemone* x *hybrida* 'Queen Charlotte'; in front, evergreen elephant's ears *Bergenia cordifolia*, with rich rose flowers, and *Helleborus orientalis*, with plum flowers, both peaking in spring.

🌸 Another winning combination, using several stalwart shrubs, is ice-pink *Lavatera* 'Barnsley', which flowers till the first frosts, and *Buddleia davidii* 'Nanho Purple', behind small dark-foliaged *Berberis thunbergii* 'Atropurpurea Nana', and *Fothergilla* 'Blue Mist'. Flank them with lily-flowered 'China Pink' tulips, burgundy ground-cover *Heuchera micrantha diversifolia* 'Palace Purple', and compact, deep pink-flowered *Geranium sanguineum*.

🌸 Classic and unbeatable: the summer border that makes everybody misty-eyed. Here's the magic formula, for you to add to and adapt as you please: old-fashioned or repeat-flowering English roses in pinks and crimsons, interspersed with wild foxglove *Digitalis purpurea* and tall bellflower *Campanula glomerata* 'Superba', which has deep lavender flower clusters; masses of old-fashioned lavender *Lavandula angustifolia*; carpeting crane's bill geraniums.

🌸 Rich purple *Buddleia davidii* 'Black Knight' is dynamite with the apricot

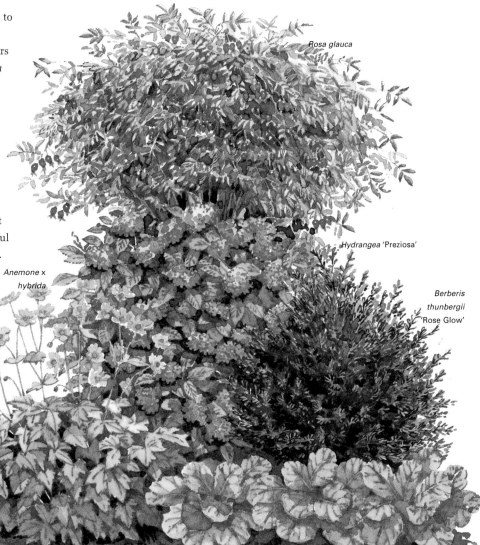

Rosa glauca

Hydrangea 'Preziosa'

Anemone x *hybrida*

Berberis thunbergii 'Rose Glow'

Bergenia cordifolia

Lonicera periclymenum
'Graham Thomas'

BEST UNDERPLANTING FOR ROSES

Ground-cover geraniums, catmint *Nepeta* x *fassenii*, lavenders, *Stachys byzantina* and lime green *Alchemilla mollis* are the classic plants to partner roses. Fresh white and yellow feverfew flowers look enchanting with the rich pink blooms of *Rosa gallica officinalis*. And for yellow roses, blue-flowered geraniums are unbeatable. Interplant rose bushes, of course, with masses of spring- and summer-flowering bulbs, especially alliums and white *Lilium regale*.

Rosa gallica
'Versicolor'

BEST EDGING PLANTS

All the following low-growers work well as a continuous border edging, or as intermittent clump planting along the border. Neat dwarf lavender *Lavandula* 'Hidcote' (for sun); perennial foamflower *Tiarella wherryi*, with pale green leaves and cream summer flowers (for shade); *Alchemilla mollis*, with lime-green rounded leaves and sulphur-yellow flower sprays in summer (for sun or part shade); *Armeria maritima*, pink-flowered grassy hummocks (for sun); evergreen dwarf box *Buxus sempervirens* 'Suffruticosa' (for sun or part shade); pinks, *Dianthus* hybrids, with gray-green leaves, small carnation flowers (for sun); golden marjoram *Origanum vulgare* 'Aureum' (for sun or part shade).

Philadelphus 'Belle Etoile'

English rose 'Abraham Darby', and a crowd of apricot foxgloves *Digitalis purpurea* 'Sutton's Apricot'. More purple-and-orange late summer frolics: classic orange tiger lilies *Lilium tigridium* among blue-violet flowers of monkshood *Aconitum napellus*, backed with softer spires of lilac-coloured *Salvia turkestanica*.

❦ For a luscious fragrant border in summer: clothe wall or fence with early flowering honeysuckle *Lonicera periclymenum* 'Graham Thomas'. In front, plant sensationally scented shrub *Philadelphus* 'Belle Etoile', which has white flowers with purple blotch at petal base, and the fine-fragranced, ancient, rose-pink and crimson-streaked *Rosa gallica* 'Versicolor'. Underplant with later-flowering white *Lilium regale*, catmint, and lavender, and for delicious evening scent, sow annuals *Nicotiana affinis* and night-scented stock *Matthiola bicornis*.

IMAGINATIVE WAYS WITH CLIMBERS

❦ Instead of cutting back a rambling rose that has grown beyond its supporting pillar or post, loop the ends back onto their stems and tie them down. You'll have a colorful 'bottle' of blooms next year.

❦ Encase drainpipes with trellis, and cover with clematis such as white 'Henryi', lavender-blue 'General Sikorski'.

❦ Add a column of colour to the border with a large painted wooden or metal obelisk, and smother with a late-flowering *Clematis viticella*.

❦ A wall of climbing roses can be underplanted with *Forsythia intermedia*, which flowers from early spring and will hide the roses' bare stems.

❦ In an open, sunny garden, create welcome dappled shade by covering a trellised pergola with climbers such as ornamental vines, roses, honeysuckle, clematis. Turn a seat into a fragrant arbor with the addition of a simple metal arch, planted at base with scented jasmine or honeysuckle.

❦ Plant *Clematis macropetala* in a tall Ali Baba jar, and its ravishing mauve flowers will cascade over the edge.

❦ Use an old garden umbrella, stripped of fabric, for a climbing frame: at its base, plant purple vine *Vitis vinifera* 'Purpurea', or deep violet *Clematis* 'Jackmanii Superba'.

❦ Pink and lemon honeysuckle flowers on their own are enchanting. With the flowers of *Clematis* 'Etoile Violette', they're sensational.

❦ Even an old ladder can serve as a host for a couple of clematis.

❦ Use the exotic to liven the humdrum: plant hardy passionflower *Passiflora caerulea* to romp through *Viburnum burkwoodii* and give it splashy fake flowers in summer.

❦ Think grand. Erect tall poles every 6ft (1.8m) or so along the garden fence, and attach thick rope between them to form elegant swags. Plant *Clematis montana*, rambling roses, *Jasminum officinale*, honeysuckle and vines at the base of poles, and coax them to shin up the poles and along the swags (one way to blot out the neighbor's washing line).

❦ Use small-flowered clematis to scramble over less-than-lively shrubs in the border: late-flowering *viticellas* with spring-flowering shrubs; early-flowering *alpinas* and *macropetalas* with later flowering shrubs. Plant 24in (60cm) away from the shrub, and guide them in the right direction with a cane. Enliven evergreens such as euonymus with clematis; consider rich red 'Madame Julia Correvon' or white 'Marie Boisselot' over conifers; yellow-flowered *C. orientalis* or soft blue *C. alpina* 'Frances Rivis' over holly. Train large-flowered hybrid clematis over large lavenders; thread double-flowered purple *viticella* varieties through rose bushes and up apple trees, for flowers and fruit at the same time.

❦ Sweet peas are perfect for scrambling over shrubs, too: deep pink perennial *Lathyrus latifolius* with purple smoke bush *Cotinus coggygria*; annual sweet peas over silver-leaved artemisias.

❦ Roses and clematis are ideal planting partners. Choose clematis which are pruned in spring, at the same time as the rose: for example, ruby *C.* 'Niobe' with strong pink *R.* 'Zéphirine Drouhin'; pale blue *C.* 'Perle d'Azur' with apricot climber *R.* 'Meg' or powder pink 'New Dawn'; purple *C.* 'Lady Betty Balfour' with yellow rose 'Golden Showers'. Yummy.

127

SPECIFICS

LIGHT UP THE SHADE

Liven a dim, dark corner with focus of stone statue or garden seat, and surround with textural, shapely greenery that thrives in shady sites. Some that fit the bill: *Fatsia japonica*, ivies, *Dryopteris* ferns, large-leaved hostas. At the back, the golden star flowers and cascading shoots of uncomplaining winter-flowering jasmine. Add light and scent in summer with pots of all-white flowers such as regale lilies, tobacco plant *Nicotiana alata*, *Impatiens*.

PLANTS IN PAVING

Make a path or paved patio look like it's been there forever, with cushions of plants billowing over hard edges. Remove mortar between slabs if necessary, replace with a mix of fine potting bark, peat and grit, and plant with soft blue *Campanula carpatica*, *Viola tricolor* (leave some seedheads to spread their seed), sweet white alyssum or chamomile for scent. Plant varieties of spreading thyme *Thymus serpyllum* into the gaps of a sunny garden path, using fast-growing upright golden and broadleaf thymes at path's edge; they'll survive stepping on, and will release their pungent fragrance. Colorful alternative for a sunny spot is a rock rose walk; plant gray- and green-leafed helianthemums in pinks, lemons, whites and reds to form a patchwork path in early summer.

RIGHT PLANT, RIGHT PROPS

Cottage garden planting calls for naive, rustic hardware: wigwams of hazel beanpoles in the border; a simple willow arch or white picket fence. By contrast, a formal garden would be more suited to wooden obelisks and filigree metal arches.

Another atmospheric tip: let honeysuckle and scented jasmine scramble romantically over the house walls. Not only does it look gorgeous, nobody can tell if you have a country cottage or suburban bungalow. All the best gardeners cheat.

USE HERBS CREATIVELY

❀ Edge a small formal herb border with dwarf box hedging *Buxus sempervirens* 'Suffruticosa', or compact, squiggly foliaged silvery gray mounds of dwarf cotton lavender *Santolina chamaecyparissus nana*. Space small plants of each 9in (22cm) apart.

❀ Make a fragrant thyme or chamomile seat by building a raised brick bed and filling with gritty compost; plant with chamomile 'Treneague' or different spreading thymes, spacing plants 4-6in (10-15cm) apart. They'll join up to form a wonderfully scented cushion.

❀ Keep herbs in their place with a brightly painted wooden cartwheel or, more originally, a painted ladder or two, laid along level ground.

TOPIARY TRICKS

Craftily clipped evergreens are an asset to every kind of garden, from cottage to formal. For large shapes, use box or yew, which can both grow up to 12in (30cm) a year. You could also use quick-growing privet, box plain and

MAKING A TOPIARY SPHERE

1 Stand above the plant and clip a broad band around its waist.
2 Clip from the top center point in segments to the waist, then clip upwards from bottom point to the waist.
3 The finished sphere; trim regularly to keep in shape.

1
2
3

variegated, shrubby honeysuckle *Lonicera nitida*, juniper, and bay for simple shapes. Trim your topiary little and often.

To make a simple topiary sphere, stand above the plant and clip around its waist, first. Round it down from the top center point in segments to the waist, then clip upwards from bottom point to waist. Keep standing back and checking from all angles; this is not a task to rush. For a cone, tie three canes together into an elongated triangle for height you want your plant to attain, and have occasional snipping sessions, using the guide each time, until the plant reaches the apex. You can also make wire mesh guides and push them over the plant, clipping any bits that poke beyond the wire. For adventurous shapes (chunky chicken, cup-and-saucer), discover the creative inner you by snipping free form. Start with a large plant, and remember, if your peacock turns into a frog, like a bad haircut it will grow again.

HOW TO MAKE A STANDARD BOX BUSH

When the plant is 24in (60cm) high, shorten the lower branches by half to form a stem, and shape the top into a rough ball shape. The following year, cut all branches from the stem; the lollipop top should be at least half the stem height. Trim to shape. For a taller stem, allow the shoots at the top of the lollipop to grow, and cut out the lower branches.

HOW TO MAKE A STANDARD FUCHSIA

Choose a vigorous bush fuchsia. Push a cane into the pot, and tie the main stem to it. Pinch out side shoots (leave the leaves) and keep pinching out as they grow. Pot up to larger size as plant

grows. When stem reaches the height you want, plus 3in (7cm), pinch out the growing tip and allow half a dozen strong shoots to develop, to form the head. Keep pinching back side shoots to encourage the formation of a bushy head. When formed, pinch out leaves on main stem. Trim flowerhead in early spring before bringing it outside.

INDISPENSABLE IVY

❀ Train several quick-growing varieties up a fence, securing the stems initially with heavy tape till they cling for themselves, and use as an evergreen backdrop for deciduous flowering climbers such as clematis.

❀ Give garden center statuary antique status by sploshing with sour milk or yoghurt to attract algae and training ivy up and around; front with ferns. Instant atmosphere.

❀ Use large-leaved, gold-splashed *Hedera colchica* 'Sulphur Heart' (hardy to Zone 6) to conceal ugly fences, walls or garden buildings; smallest bird's foot ivies to grow over wire topiary shapes. Make your own heart-in-a-pot by bending a

Standard box bushes add a different shape and texture to the border, and make the eye pause. These small-scale specimens are ideal for creating detailed interest by the garden gate.

IVY CIRCLES

Common ivy can be highly decorative if you train it into formal shapes. Coax young plants, with the help of bent hair pins, to grow around wire hoops or arches against a wall, and trim to keep in shape.

coathanger into a heart shape, pushing the hook part into the compost and planting a bird's foot ivy alongside. Finish off with a layer of moss tucked round.

❀ Create illusion with ivy: train around a sequence of wire arches flat against a wall, or around large wire hoops attached to wall.

Now it's your turn to dream up your own ideal plant partners. After all, who am I to dictate how you create your own earthly paradise, plant for plant? Great gardens were not created with endless rules and regulations. So go ahead with your own highly personal vision. Indulge yourself with the plants that appeal to you in color and form, giving them places where they'll thrive, and raising them right. If you do nothing other than that, your garden will be a winner, and the place you'll want to be more than anywhere else in the world. Go out there, and have a rollicking good time.

WHAT CAN GO WRONG

Sooner or later you are going to have to deal with disease in the garden, and worse yet, a death. This is not to be taken personally. However, a little knowledge might help to prevent a similar occurrence. Pests and diseases are daunting, and especially hard for the beginner to diagnose and deal with. If you're a hypochondriac, you'll look up your black-blotched leaf in a book and find it has twenty-five diseases, all of them fatal. Start out with the comfort that no garden is pest or disease free; this can save you much anguish. Your plot isn't a sterile showcase, but is full of living things and casualties are inevitable. That said, don't let pests build up on plants. Cut out any diseased or damaged parts pronto. Grow the healthiest plants you can, and they'll prove more resilient. Throw out chemical sprays which upset the garden's ecosystem and pave the way for more pests. Put up physical barriers. Practice preventative measures. Above all, be patient: it takes time to build up a balanced ecology in the garden so that predator feeds off its natural pest – the ideal you should be striving for.

131

WHY PLANTS DIE ON YOU

Some people believe that if a garden doesn't like a plant, it throws the plant out. I need a more concrete reason. An ailing plant doesn't necessarily mean that a pest or disease has struck it down. Weather is the number one killer. Frost, drought, fierce, freezing winds and snow can do irreparable damage.

Gardeners who are forgetful about watering play their part in killing off plants. Likewise, those who place a sun-loving plant in deep shade or a bog plant in a dry border.

Many plants and trees die through lack of water when they are trying to get established in their first season. Waterlogged ground is another culprit. And growing plants too closely together inevitably results in some thriving, while others suffer.

DEFICIENCIES

In soil rich in organic matter, plants with nutritional deficiencies are unusual; the plants have all that they need. Symptoms of deficiency in minerals appear as blotches on leaves, yellow patches, brittle stems and deformities, and are hard for the first-time gardener to identify and therefore correct. Safest treatment, then, is broad-based. Mulch, spray plants with liquid seaweed or feed with fish emulsion, and you will provide them with all the trace elements they need.

ROGUES GALLERY OF PESTS

Impossible, and too discouraging, to feature all the garden's plant pests, but these are the chief chafers and chompers. The prognosis isn't dismal, so long as plants are healthy to start with. There is much you can do to lessen armies of garden pests. Rotate crops each season, water regularly and grow vegetables under clear plastic tarp to cut down on pest attacks.

APHIDS Greenfly and blackfly win prizes for persistence and aren't fussy about what they pester. They suck sap, weaken plants, and transmit viruses too. *Symptoms:* Visible on stem and bud, which is sometimes distorted; leaves often have holes. Blackfly crowd stems of ornamentals, roses, some vegetables. Sticky deposits attract black sooty mould. Woolly aphids attack fruit trees and vines, depositing what looks like white candy floss. *Strategy:* Rub off with fingers and jet spray with water. Spray with soft soap insecticide or derris early on as aphids appear on the stem; spray fruit trees just before or after flowering. Keep numbers down so that later, when beneficials emerge – ladybugs, hoverfly, lacewings, spiders, ants – they can take over. Grow cool weather veggies in autumn to make them less vulnerable to attack in spring; and grow open flowers amongst vegetables to attract hoverflies, predators of aphids.

BLACK VINE WEEVIL Don't chuck used compost on to beds to bulk up soil without checking first for these horrible little grubs. You may be introducing the virulent vine weevil to its new home. *Symptoms:* Larvae feed on roots of plants in pots and ground. Adults work above ground, chomping leaves of shrubs, rhododendrons, vines, too. *Strategy:* Biological control (*see Pests and Predators, p. 138*). Look for white grubs when repotting.

CABBAGE MAGGOTS *Symptoms:* Plants don't grow, then wilt. *Strategy:* Dig up and destroy; dig over site in winter to expose cocoons. Next time use physical barriers (*see p. 138*).

CATERPILLARS *Symptoms:* A skeletal shrub where yesterday stood a healthy one. Also, chunky holes in leaves, defoliated shrubs, even trees. *Strategy:* Pick off when seen, spray plants with *Bacillus thuringiensis*, a bacterium which exclusively kills caterpillars.

CATS Personally speaking, cocoa shells seem to be the only deterrent, and only when they're new. By the way, gravel says one thing to cats: litter tray.

CODLING MOTH A grade one pest, also known as apple and pear maggot. *Symptoms:* Caterpillars tunnel into fruit and feed from inside, leaving brown powdery mess on outside. *Preventive strategy:* Tree traps (*see p. 138*).

CUTWORMS, CHAFER GRUBS, LEATHERJACKETS, WIREWORMS Little grubs and worms eat baby plants, especially brassicas, below ground; cutworms attack at ground level. *Strategy:* Dig over ground in winter for birds. Keep ground weed-free. Push sections of plastic bottles deeply into soil over plant or seedling; protect plants with collars. Biological control available (*see p. 138*).

DEER A common garden pest throughout most of the country, are fond of beheading roses, daylilies, you name it. Fences 8–10ft (2.5-3m) high are the only sure fire deterrent.

EARWIGS *(see Battle Tactics).*

EUROPEAN APPLE SAWFLY After snacking on surface, larvae then burrow into apples. *Symptoms:* Large, twirly scars on fruit. *Strategy:* Gather and destroy fallen apples. Next time spray with rotenone, when petals have fallen.

EELWORM and **NARCISSUS BULB FLY** attack bulbs. *Symptoms:* Bulb is soft, rotten. When cut open, dark rings are apparent. *Strategy:* No cure. Throw away infected bulbs and don't plant bulbs for several years on same patch.

FLEA BEETLE *Symptoms:* Many small holes in leaves of cabbages as well as radish, turnips. *Strategy:* Spray with derris. Next time grow crops under protective plastic tarp.

GOPHERS, WOODCHUCKS eat, eat, eat, and all on your patch. *Strategy:* Wire netting 36in (90cm) high, buried at least 12-18in (30-45cm) into the ground, is the only deterrent. Protect trees with plastic tree guards.

GYPSY MOTH Caterpillars over-winter in large colonies in a nest of silken webbing. They feed voraciously on trees of all kinds. *Strategy:* Burn nests, sticky traps. *(see Battle Tactics).*

JAPANESE BEETLE Coppery green beetle eats from July through September. *Strategy:* Hand-pick into can of soapy water. Infect larvae with milky spore virus.

LEAF MINER GRUBS tunnel into leaves of many plant varieties especially chrysanthemums. *Strategy:* Pick off affected leaves.

LEAF-ROLLING SAWFLY *Symptoms:* Rolled rose leaves. Left alone, the sawfly larvae nestling within will destroy the leaves. *Strategy:* Pick off and destroy leaves right away. Spray with rotenone.

MEXICAN BEAN BEETLES *Symptoms:* Notches in leaves of broad beans, peas. *Strategy:* If problem on young plants is severe, use rotenone.

MICE eat crocus, clematis, pea and bean seeds, for starters. You can buy humane mice traps and release mice in safe sites, but try mothballs. Plant out peas and beans as seedlings.

MOLES like to make mountains out of their molehills in lawns and vegetable patches. *Strategy:* Traps and smoke-outs are available, but they're not nice. If problem is really severe, try expensive but effective device which sends high-frequency soundwaves through tunnels.

ONION MAGGOT *Symptoms:* Leaves of onions and leeks wilt, turn yellow. Closer scrutiny reveals white maggots at plant base. *Strategy:* Dig up and destroy affected plants. Dig over larvae-infested earth in winter. Grow plants under protective tarp, or dust rotenone between seedling rows.

PEA MOTH *Symptoms:* Caterpillars in pea pods. *Strategy:* Dig over earth in winter. Next time cover plants when flowering with fleece; sow early to avoid mid-summer moth onslaught.

PEAR MIDGE Larvae invade fruit when tiny. *Symptoms:* Fruitlets turn black, fall off. *Strategy:* Destroy affected fruitlets, looking out for ones still on tree. Dig over earth in winter to expose cocoons for birds.

PLUM SAWFLY *Symptoms:* Larvae eat the fruit from inside, which causes them to fall. *Strategy:* Destroy fallen fruitlets. Spray trees with rotenone when petals fall.

RED SPIDER MITE Their favourite plant is datura (I speak from experience.) Also attack berries and figs and other fruits in hot, dry weather. *Symptoms:* Leaves look like the goodness has been sucked out of them. (It has, and does the fruit no favors). Use magnifying lens to see the minuscule mites on underside. *Strategy:* Remove infested leaves; mist frequently with water to make conditions less hospitable. Biological control available *(see p. 138).* Spray with rotenone if severe.

ROOT APHIDS attack the roots of lettuce and other plants. *Symptoms:* Plants wilt and may die. *Strategy:* Grow resistant varieties, as in lettuce 'Titania'.

ROOT MAGGOT *Symptoms:* Larvae leave tunnels in carrots, parsnips, celery, celeriac and parsley; often fungus disease takes over. *Strategy:* Dig up affected plants. Next time use a physical barrier *(see p. 138).* Sow earlier carrots which are more likely to miss root maggot's calling card.

SCALE INSECTS More sap suckers, but small and flat, on fruit trees, vines. *Symptoms:* Disfigured leaves, honeydew and possibly sooty black mould. *Strategy:* Spray with insecticidal soft soap.

SLUGS AND SNAILS In damp, warm weather, out they come, nibbling their way through your entire plant collection. Slugs and snails especially love delphiniums (plant them in spring; it's safer), hollyhocks, hostas, lupins, clematis, and bedding plants, but mostly avoid aromatic herbs and prickly, rough-textured plants as well as

133

ground-cover geraniums and pulmonaria. *Symptoms:* Range from small bites to major meals. *Strategy:* Don't throw slugs and snails over the garden fence, they'll only come back to haunt you, leaving a tell-tale trail of slime. Instead, stamp hard on snails, throw slugs into a bucket of salted water, or throw both into the garden pond for frog or toad. Rout them out at night with a torch and pick them up after rain. Dig over soil to expose them to predators (birds, frogs, toads, hedgehogs). Trap and obstruct them or use a biological slug killer (*see p. 138*). The only acceptable organic slug killer is aluminium sulfate.

SQUIRRELS Only when you see a squirrel sitting on your fence, eating an entire pear from your tree, can you grasp its blatant audacity. Digging up and demolition of bulbs are the squirrel's speciality. *Strategy:* Wire netting to protect vulnerable subjects is the only effective course of action.

WHITEFLY Serious in greenhouse, less so outdoors, but they love brassicas. *Symptoms:* White scales on plants; knock leaves, and hoards of them fly up. *Strategy:* Remove lower leaves where larvae congregate. Spray with insecticidal soft soap.

WOODLICE Love dead plants, live plants, damaged plants. *Symptom:* Big, uneven holes in leaves. *Strategy:* Don't leave plant debris, empty pots and boxes lying around.

ROGUE'S GALLERY OF DISEASES

Plant diseases are fungal, viral or bacterial, and you will see less of all three if you practice good gardening. Don't leave dead wood or plant debris lying around. Deal with weeds promptly. Disinfect pots and seed trays at season's end. Rotate vegetable crops. Choose disease-resistant varieties of vegetables, ornamentals, roses, fruit bushes and fruit trees where possible.

Despite all precautions, even in the world's finest soil, some diseases will rear up, one or two more troublesome than others. And you might find a certain disease will sweep your neighborhood in one season, like a new flu strain. Always disinfect tools after use on diseased plants. And give weakened plants foliar seaweed feed to boost recovery.

APPLE AND PEAR CANKER *Symptoms:* Sunken, swollen patches on bark; white fungus in summer. *Strategy:* Cut back affected branches to clean wood. Spray with Bordeaux mixture after fruit is harvested.

APPLE AND PEAR SCAB *Symptoms:* Brown scabby marks on fruit and leaves, although fruit is still edible. *Strategy:* Prune out affected shoots. Spray with sulfur and soft soap fungicide when flower buds are first formed, and at frequent intervals. Grow scab-resistant varieties of fruits such as 'MacFree' (apples) and 'Moonglow' (pears).

APPLE BITTER ROT *Symptoms:* Brown, rotten fruit with mold patches; fruit falls eventually. *Strategy:* Pick off and destroy affected fruit as this disease spreads fast in humid Southern areas.

BACTERIAL CANKER Major killer of plums, peaches, nectarines, almonds and cherries, as well as their ornamental varieties. *Symptoms:* Depressions at branch base and stems in autumn or winter; in spring they enlarge. On cherry, can exude orange-coloured gum. Brown spots on foliage as summer progresses. *Strategy:* Prune out infected areas. Spray with Bordeaux mixture in mid-summer and monthly until autumn.

BITTER PIT *Symptoms:* Affects apples, causing indentations on the skin and brown patches beneath. *Strategy:* Destroy affected fruit. Also helpful to keep water supply regular.

BLACKSPOT *Symptoms:* A bad attack on a rose bush looks awful. Sickly, yellowing leaves, falling off, are blighted with big black marks. *Strategy:* Remove all diseased leaves from bush and ground, burning or binning them. At first sign of attack, spray with garden fungicide of sulfur and soft soap. Some roses are more susceptible than others, so grow disease-resistant varieties. Give rose bushes space, and keep open at center.

BLOSSOM-END ROT *Symptoms:* Squash and zucchini show up rotten, the first indication being that the blossom end fails to develop fully. Also similar: tomato blossom-end rot. *Strategy:* Keep soil sweet by addition of lime, allow plenty of space so plants do not touch one another. Use high phosphorus, low nitrogen potash fertilizer, 5:10:5 is perfect.

BLOSSOM WILT Affects tree fruit blossom. *Symptoms:* Flowers wither but do not drop; shoots and leaves die. *Strategy:* Prune out infection and remove all affected parts.

BOTRYTIS BLIGHT The scourge of geraniums, petunias, peonies. *Symptoms:* leaves turn black and fall off. *Strategy:* Give plants plenty of air circulation, keep foliage dry. Like most fungi, botrytis loves damp conditions. Best prevention is to clean away all leaves and garden rubbish at the end of the season, as botrytis overwinters in debris.

BROWN ROT Common in tree fruit. *Symptoms:* Brown, soft fruit with creamy pustules. Hangs on tree all winter. *Strategy:* Prune out infection; remove all diseased fruits or they will set up infection for next year.

CLUB ROOT No mistaking this attacker of cabbages and wallflowers. *Symptoms:* Distortion of roots which eventually rot. *Strategy:* Dig out, destroy, and in future grow in different, well-limed (club root only strikes acid soil) and well-drained site. Never return to previous site as the disease stays in soil for years. Helpful, too, to grow brassicas in pots so sound root system can be built up; transplant at late stage.

FIREBLIGHT Serious bacterial disease affecting pears, late-flowering apples, shrubs. *Symptoms:* Flowers and leaves die; plant looks scorched. Areas of distorted bark may ooze slime in spring. *Strategy:* Prune out infection; in severe cases remove whole tree.

FOOT AND ROOT ROT Fungal disease frequently carried in compost. *Symptoms:* Stem base blackens. *Strategy:* Destroy affected plants. Don't use old compost.

LEAF SPOTS Fungal disease of leaves at its worst in rose blackspot. *Symptoms:* spots and blotches of assorted shapes and sizes. *Strategy:* Pick off and destroy affected leaves. Spray regularly with Bordeaux mixture.

MILDEWS Downy or powdery – the result's the same: a debilitating fungus on ornamental plants, fruit trees, bushes, lettuce. If it's rampant on your Michaelmas daisies, grow varieties that are less prone to mildew, such as asters from the *novae-angliae* group. Some lettuce are resistant too. Don't grow roses too close to warm walls. Mildews thrive in humid, plant-packed situations. *Symptoms:* Powdery white or gray mildew on leaves, stems, fruit. *Strategy:*

Spray with Bordeaux mixture. Pick off affected parts where possible. Don't plant vegetables and fruit bushes too closely, keep soil weed-free, and don't overwater. Rotate crops.

PEACH LEAF CURL Attacks peach, nectarine and almond trees. *Symptoms:* Leaves develop red blisters and pucker, then drop off. *Strategy:* On fan-trained trees, roll plastic sheeting across in early spring to protect from spores that cause disease. Spray with Bordeaux mixture in late winter as preventative.

POTATO SCAB Skin disease of potatoes, result of growing in too alkaline soil. Also affects sweet potatoes. *Strategy:* To acidify soil, add sulfur at the rate of one half pound (225g) over the surface of a 15ft (4.5m) row to lower pH to between 4.5 and 5.5.

RASPBERRY CANE SPOT AND BLIGHT *Symptoms:* Cane spot has small purple spots which spread and split, while cane blight forms brown patches at base of canes; leaves and buds shrivel up. *Strategy:* Cut out affected canes and destroy. Next time, spray with organic fungicide or Bordeaux mixture at onset of first flowers.

RUST Serious disease that affects fruit trees as well as wide variety of ornamental plants and roses. Hollyhocks get rust so badly that you may want to grow similar, less troublesome lavatera instead. *Symptoms:* Spots on leaves in rusty shades from yellow to brown. *Strategy:* Remove affected leaves immediately; use fungicide spray of sulfur and soft soap.

SCALD Looks like a disease, but actually the result of injury from too intense sunlight on tender growth of tomatoes, peppers, eggplant. In the northern hemisphere, the south side of a newly planted tree will scald as well. *Symptoms:* Brownish irregular spots on the upper surface. *Strategy:* Grow tomatoes

in cages so fruits are shaded by leaves from direct sun. Shade newly planted veggies and trees for first few days.

SILVER LEAF Affects deciduous shrubs and trees, especially plum and cherry. *Symptoms:* Leaves develop silvery sheen and affected branch dies back. Fungal growths appear on dead wood. *Strategy:* Prune out dead branches and twigs in summer, cutting back 5-10cm (2-4in) beyond infection. If there is no sign of improvement, the tree must be cut down.

STONE FRUIT BACTERIAL SPOT Fungus which attacks ornamentals as well as peaches, plums. *Symptoms:* Bright pink or red spots on stems and branches, prevalent in damp weather. *Strategy:* Prune out infected areas.

VIRUS DISEASES Think hard. Was that plant always variegated? *Symptoms:* Distortion, stunted growth, yellowing, mottled or streaked leaves. Where possible buy virus-free strains. *Strategy:* Dig up and destroy. Plant replacements on different site.

WILT Actually a fungus. *Symptom:* Speedy collapse of clematis as well as asters, peonies. *Strategy:* Cut out all wilted shoots or dig up plant if necessary. Plant clematis in garden 6in (15cm) deeper than soil level in pot, so if struck down, new shoots will hopefully emerge.

PREVENTING PESTS AND DISEASE

SPRING

1 Sow marigolds and fried egg plant, on vegetable patch, too, to bring in hoverflies.

2 Keep greenfly and other aphids down by rubbing off with fingers, and jet water spray, so beneficials can take over later, in summer.

3 Apply fresh grease bands around fruit trees.

4 Protect seedlings from slugs with plastic barriers, and young crops from pests with plastic tarp.

5 Sow carrots early to avoid root maggot. Further thwart it by erecting a polythene wall, which should be at least 3ft (90cm) in height, around crops.

6 Strengthen plants with regular foliar feed of dilute seaweed solution or fish emulsion.

7 Protect cabbage from root maggot with individual collars.

8 Pick caterpillars and their eggs off plants by hand; keep look out for destructive cabbage white.

SUMMER

1 Keep on top of weeds: hoe, hoe, quick quick hoe.

2 Net fruit bushes to protect from birds.

3 If slugs are a problem, water nematode solution into beds and borders.

4 Hang pheromone traps in apple and pear trees to trap male codling moths.

5 Keep up a steady watering program to produce vigorous plants that can shrug off disease.

6 Continue to foliar feed regularly.

7 If vine weevil or soil insects are a problem, use biological control.

8 Spray aphid-prone roses and plants with soft soap insecticide.

AUTUMN

1 Clean area around rose bushes so blackspot spores don't overwinter.

2 Replace old fruit bushes with certified virus-free stock.

3 Gather autumn leaves for leafmold.

4 Protect buds of fruit trees and bushes, where practical, from birds. Use broad mesh netting.

5 Dig over earth to expose overwintering soil pests to their predators as well as to the weather.

WINTER

1 Apply grease bands around fruit tree trunks to prevent female wingless moth climbing into trees to lay her eggs.

2 Dig up and destroy carrot root and brassica stems to get rid of any pests or their larvae.

3 Remove any withered fruit still on trees as it will harbor spores for next season.

4 Check blackcurrant bushes for signs of big bud, removing any buds that are swollen. Net against bullfinches, which eat buds.

5 Cover peach, almond and nectarine trees with polythene barrier to protect against rain which carries peach leaf curl fungus. Keep covered till mid-spring. Alternatively spray with Bordeaux mixture.

ORGANIC GARDENING

PESTS AND PREDATORS

Some pest armies can be best dealt with by calling in the cavalry. Biological control – where you offload natural predators onto their prey – is the way of the future, and it's available now.

SLUGS Applied correctly, this treatment is 100 per cent effective, and I've found lasts longer than the six weeks the manufacturers suggest. All you do is dilute several million parasitic nematodes with water, and water the solution onto beds and borders. The nematodes slip into the slug, poisoning it slowly until it disintegrates. No need to feel bad about it. These predators are already present in the ground; you're just giving nature a helping hand.

RED SPIDER MITE *Phytoseiulis persimilis* feeds on eggs and insects both; most useful in greenhouse.

BLACK VINE WEEVIL You can use, on affected soil or compost, a solution containing millions of nematodes that will rid you of vine weevils and other destructive soil pests such as leatherjackets, cutworms and chafer grubs. Only effective in summer months.

WHITEFLY There is a control available for whitefly, but only in the greenhouse. The predator to ask for is parasitic wasp *Encarsia formosa*.

SAWDUST, JAM AND OTHER BATTLE TACTICS

❀ **USE YOUR HANDS TO PICK OFF PESTS**

❀ **TRAP FRUIT-GUZZLING WASPS** in a jam jar. Mix blob of jam with water, make foil lid with small hole.

❀ **KEEP AWAY CABBAGE MAGGOTS** by preventing the female laying eggs. Chop felt into squares, snip each to the center, fit snugly around plant stems.

❀ **CONFOUND THE ROOT MAGGOT** by making barriers too high for this low-flying pest. Wind plastic sheeting, at least 75cm (30in) high, round four canes at corners of carrot crop. Alternatively, grow carrots under lightweight spun plastic tarp that allows in water and sun but keeps insects out.

❀ **PREVENT CODLING MOTH AND PLUM SAWFLY** spoiling your fruit by hanging sticky traps in trees. The male moth is attracted by the sexual attractant on the trap, and gets stuck. This puts a crimp in moth mating, as you might imagine. Hang traps in trees in early summer.

❀ **DON'T PLANT IN BLOCKS** because you'll encourage that plant's particular pest to come and feast.

❀ **KEEP WINTER MOTH CATERPILLARS FROM FRUIT TREES** by placing grease bands around trunks, 30-90cm (1-3ft) from base; leave till mid-spring. The wingless female pupae crawl up trunks to lay their eggs, and will get trapped on sticky surface.

❀ **SCARE BIRDS OFF CROPS** by stretching old cassette tapes or black cotton taut across crops.

❀ **FOOL THE FOE** by planting onions and carrots together, thus killing two birds with one stone, or two pests with one ploy. Carrot and onion flies get confused by this intercropping.

❀ **DETER SLUGS AND SNAILS** with physical barriers. Try cut-off plastic beverage bottle over baby plants and salad crops; sharp-edged grit around plants (slugs hate sliding over jagged edges); sawdust, soot or ash. Entice them to their death with heaps of damp bran covered with cabbage leaves, or orange shells left for them to crawl under. Pots of beer sunk into the ground kill beneficial pests too.

THE GREEN FACTOR

Using chemical sprays often increases pests and diseases in the garden, never mind the damage they do to their immediate environment and beyond. But although the word 'spray' has chemical connotations, some sprays are in fact, completely organic.

PYRETHRUM Extracted from chrysanthemum, but available only with a chemical synergist. Pyrethrum kills many insect pests, including small caterpillars, but also kills some beneficial insects, so only use as a last resort. Don't use near ponds as it can kill fish, frogs, toads.

ROTENONE Plant extract in liquid or powder form. Slower-acting than pyrethrum, and as indiscriminating, so use with caution.

PIRIMICARB insecticide for killing aphids is not billed as organic, but is worth knowing about because it won't harm beneficial insects, except possibly ladybug larvae.

SOFT SOAP insecticides kill soft-bodied insects only, but are harmful to larvae of ladybugs and hoverfly. Useful to keep aphids from building up. Harmful to fish, so don't use near ponds. Can also scorch young foliage.

BORDEAUX MIXTURE is the traditional fungicide of copper sulphate and slaked lime. Although not strictly speaking organic, Bordeaux mixture is not harmful to garden life. Coats leaves with invisible protective layer, so wash sprayed fruit before eating.

SULFUR is an effective, organic fungicide, incorporated with soft soap as a garden fungicide spray. Not to be sprayed near fish. Some ferns, gooseberry and grape varieties have adverse reactions to sulfur.

DEALING WITH WEEDS

A seedling by any other name, sure, but don't wait too long before deciding whether it qualifies as weed or welcome addition; by then it could have taken over your garden. Experience will tell you whether you are digging up a potential tap-rooting invader or future oriental poppy.

Best policy to keep weeds under control is to hoe regularly when soil is dry. Mulches around plants and trees prevent weeds coming up, and ground-cover plants crowd out the competition.

Annual weeds, if dealt with promptly, aren't tricky to eradicate; use hand or hoe, and be vigilant. Perennial weeds are a tougher proposition. You'll need to wrench out creeping stems and dig out questing tap roots. Many of them reproduce themselves from just a tiny piece of plant left in the ground, so ban them from your compost heap or you could be cooking up trouble.

On the lawn, use a long trowel to rout out rosette-forming weeds and use a weeding knife for deep-rooters like dandelions.

If you're plagued with weeds or grass in paving cracks and paths, push them out permanently. Fill in the holes with cement or do what I did and expand them, making planting holes of compost and grit, for thymes and rock roses.

Remove top layer of compost of container-grown plants before planting; they often house weeds that might be new additions to your garden.

ANNUAL WEEDS

CHICKWEED Hoe when you see seedlings, but if you have masses of the stuff, pull up the whole weed.

COMMON BURDOCK Hoe fresh plants and dig up old ones. It can be spread round the garden, by you: those rough seeds stick to clothing.

GROUNDSEL Prolific seeder; keep at it.

HAIRY BITTERCRESS This weed has an explosive mechanism that sends seeds flying. Frequently arrives via potted plants. Hoe or hand-weed.

MEADOW GRASS Soft-leaved grass with ample seedheads; can be tricky to pull out. Persevere.

SHEPHERD'S PURSE Seeds without cessation, so be remorseless.

PERENNIAL WEEDS

BINDWEED A rampant strangler. Dig up each and every last piece of root as you come across it, and unwrap the stems that relentlessly twirl themselves around your prized plants.

BRAMBLES Blackberries they're not. Brambles go deep down and can be a menace. Cut down from above soil and dig deep to get at those roots.

BROAD-LEAVED DOCK A rooter and a seeder. Dig out those fleshy roots before it takes over.

COUCH GRASS Spreads by underground stems and seed. Dig up couch as it appears, getting out every last piece unless you want it to spread.

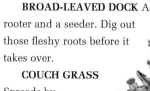

CREEPING THISTLE Tall thistle with deep roots that spreads like wildfire, but can be easily dug out.

DANDELION Ignore those who tell you that dandelions are lovely, the French eat the leaves, etc. They're a menace. Dig out every last bit of root, and never let plants seed unless you want a dandelion lawn.

GROUND ELDER Smothering with black plastic is what ground elder deserves. Otherwise, dig out every last bit of those creeping white stems, because each piece will turn into a new plant.

HORSETAIL Aptly named, with deep roots that are difficult to get out completely. Hoe to keep under control.

JAPANESE BAMBOO Pray it's not in your garden. An oriental speciality with spreading stems that go deep down. Cut back to ground level, and dig out what you can, working from the outside in.

STINGING NETTLE Although a clump of this garden weed provides a breeding site for butterflies, you may not care for it in your herbaceous border. Cut back plants (use gloves); dig out roots.

From top left: dock, thistle, bindweed, dandelion, ground elder, horsetail.

139

Often it's the simplest ideas that are the most effective. Sweet peas trained in the traditional manner and grown in a pot make a charming summer focal point.

ACKNOWLEDGMENTS

The publisher thanks the following photographers and organizations for their kind permission to reproduce the photographs in this book:

4-5 Jerry Harpur (Owner: Mrs Dymond);
6-7 Marianne Majerus (Designer: Mirabel Osler);
8-9 Jerry Harpur (Designer: Helen Yemm);
10 Marie O'Hara;
12 Linda Burgess/The Garden Picture Library;
14 Juliette Wade (Owners: Mr & Mrs Garten);
15 Andrew Lawson;
16 Neil Campbell-Sharp;
21 Derek St. Romaine;
22-23 Jane Gifford;
24 Clive Nichols (Designer: Sue Berger);
25 Noel Kavanagh;
26 Jerry Harpur (Keeyla Meadows, San Francisco);
27 Clive Nichols;
29 Hugh Palmer;
31 Howard Rice/The Garden Picture Library;
32 Marie Claire Maison/Claire de Virieu (Stylist: Sonia Laroze);
33 Marianne Majerus;
34 Clive Nichols (Hadspen Garden and Nursery, Castle Cary, Somerset);
35 David Askham/The Garden Picture Library;
36 right Clive Nichols;
36 left Clive Nichols;
37 Marianne Majerus (Designer: Beth Chatto);
40 Brigitte Thomas/The Garden Picture Library;
41 J.S. Sira/The Garden Picture Library;
42 Clay Perry/The Garden Picture Library;
43 Marianne Majerus;
44 Clive Nichols (Wolfson College, Oxford);
46 S & O Mathews;
47 John Glover (Designer: Derek Jarman);
49 Juliette Wade;
56 Clive Nichols (University Botanic Garden, Cambridge);
57 Gary Rogers/The Garden Picture Library;
58 Brigitte Thomas/The Garden Picture Library;
66-67 Mayer/le Scanff/The Garden Picture Library;
69 John Glover;
71 Jerry Harpur;
72 Clive Nichols (Vale End, Surrey);
75 Nicole & Patrick Mioulane (Landscape designer: Timothy Vaughan/Mise au Point);
76 Andrew Lawson;
78 Juliette Wade (Owner: Mrs D. Holmes);
80-81 Derek St. Romaine;
83 John Glover;
90-91 Neil Campbell-Sharp;
92 John Glover/The Garden Picture Library;
93 Derek St. Romaine;
94 Neil Holmes/The Garden Picture Library;
95 Neil Holmes/The Garden Picture Library;
96 Jane Gifford;
100 Jerry Harpur (Designer: Simon Hopkinson);
101 Jerry Harpur (Designer: Simon Hopkinson);
103 Marianne Majerus (Designer: Peter Aldington, Turn End);
105 Juliette Wade;
106 John Glover/The Garden Picture Library;
107 Michael Howes/The Garden Picture Library;
108-109 Noel Kavanagh;
111 Marianne Majerus;
112 Neil Holmes/The Garden Picture Library;
114 Marie O'Hara;
115 Jane Gifford;
116-117 Clive Nichols (East Lambrook Manor, Somerset);
118 Andrew Lawson (Designer: Anne Dexter);
119 Marianne Majerus (Designer: Mark Brown);
120 Pierre Hussenot/Cote Sud/Elizabeth Whiting & Associates;
122 Noel Kavanagh;
123 Marie O'Hara (Designer: Jane Fearnley-Whittingstall);
124 Marie O'Hara;
129 Derek St Romaine (Designer: Cleve West, Hampton Court 1994);
130-131 Clive Nichols (Mill House, Hildenborough, Kent);
140 Clive Nichols (Vale End, Surrey)